# THE PULLING

Adele Dumont is an Australian writer and critic. Her work has appeared in *Griffith Review*, *Meanjin*, *Southerly*, *ABR*, and *Sydney Review of Books*. Adele's first book, *No Man is an Island*, is an account of her experiences teaching English to asylum seekers in detention. Adele lives in Sydney, where she works as an English language teacher and examiner. When she needs a break from text and from screens, she enjoys baking, bushwalking, and eavesdropping.

# THE PULLING

ADELE DUMONT

ESSAYS

SCRIBE
Melbourne | London | Minneapolis

Scribe Publications
18–20 Edward St, Brunswick, Victoria 3056, Australia
2 John St, Clerkenwell, London, WC1N 2ES, United Kingdom
3754 Pleasant Ave, Suite 100, Minneapolis, Minnesota 55409, USA

Published by Scribe 2024



Typeset in Portrait Text by the publishers

Printed and bound in the UK by CPI Group (UK) Ltd, Croydon CR0 4YY

Scribe is committed to the sustainable use of natural resources and the use of paper products made responsibly from those resources.

978 1 922585 91 2 (Australian edition)
978 1 914484 83 4 (UK edition)
978 1 761385 49 0 (ebook)

Catalogue records for this book are available from the National Library of Australia and the British Library.

scribepublications.com.au
scribepublications.co.uk
scribepublications.com

*She was shy, and she suffered. For one thing, she bit her nails,*
*and had a cruel consciousness in her fingertips, a shame,*
*an exposure. Out of all proportion, this shame haunted her.*

D.H. LAWRENCE

# CONTENTS

# FINGERNAILS

I've always resented the fact my hands don't tell the full story. Looking at them, anyone would think I had no self-respect, or that there must be something *wrong* with me. My hands betray me. I've learned to keep them tucked away in my lap, my fingers permanently curled up in loose fists. I hold my pen and my fork in a specific, clumsy way that reveals as little of my nails as possible. Still now, if I try to hold my fingers out dead straight it feels forced and weird.

Now, as I write you this, the pad of my left middle finger has positioned itself directly above my ring finger, just to stroke the naked nail bed, exposed as new wood under old bark, a thing obscene. Now, when I scour my childhood for some kind of sign of what was yet to befall me, it is my fingernails – ravaged and tender – that are the constant. It is my fingernails that expressed what my three-and-a-half-decade-old tongue still hasn't learned how to.

Sometimes – often actually – when I'm inspecting my

nails or admiring someone else's I fantasise about stopping, at having hands like a regular person. I think about how long it would take, and how stupidly slowly nails grow. But then in quick succession after that thought comes this one: that those hands wouldn't really be *mine*. A friend once called my legs 'autobiographical' since they contained so many small marks and scratches. My dad (Papa, I mean – he can't stand the word 'dad') would always say you can't trust a man with no scars. To have normal-looking nails would feel very much its own disguise.

I can't remember ever having hands that didn't need to be concealed. Even from my own mother I tried my hardest to hide them. You'd think she'd grow inured to the sight, but when every few months she'd inevitably catch a glimpse of them, the same sigh of weary disappointment would issue from her: 'Oh Adele, your *nails*.' She'd make an example of my sister's nails, because even as a kid E kept her nails nice. Back then she used to suck two of her fingers – she'd go to sleep with them shoved right up inside her mouth, so that there were permanent indentations just below her knuckles. The dentist told us my sister should quit because it might make her teeth buck, and I forget how she quit but she did, or maybe she just eventually grew out of the habit. Then when she got a bit older she'd paint her nails crimson or black, and she accumulated mythical-looking rings set with emeralds, garnets, onyx. Papa used to say people with tattoos were stupid, but that was back in the nineties, back before my sister started tattooing her body, her fingers, too, with hand-drawn mandalas and leaves and serpents. My sister was never as conscious as I was about pleasing our parents. In the right light you might notice faint white lines on her lower wrists, but unlike me with my fingernails, she makes little attempt to hide the traces of her harm.

My mother used to tell me I'd never be able to get a job in a shop with 'hands like that'. More than once, she suggested I take up smoking (a habit she herself had quit cold turkey in her early twenties on meeting my father, because he couldn't bear the smell). I don't know how many times she said it, but I remember her using the word 'claws' to talk about my hands; even then, I wouldn't give her the satisfaction of reacting. From a very young age I'd perfected an expression of blankness. (Perhaps it's this expression that explains why, time and time again, people have described my face as 'innocent'. It's the kind of face that *Big Issue* sellers latch onto, and that means that people not much older than me like to take me under their wing, and that young children instinctively trust.) I have always felt too much, and been troubled by very small things, and I think I was tired of her telling me not to 'turn on the tears'. When I was a teenager, she'd joke to my sister: 'we'll have to take her to get *hypnotised*', or 'we should send her to see a *psychologist*!' We all understood that such suggestions were not to be taken seriously, since they were made in the same frivolous tone as when she'd speculate that with all her cats, my sister might grow up to be a lion-tamer. I guess she thought that growing my nails was just one of the things on the list that needed to be done, along with making my bed, cleaning the mouse cages, or emptying the compost. When her various attempts failed, sometimes there'd be other, gentler strategies: in among the groceries she'd bring home a bottle of that foul-tasting nail biting deterrent and with faux casualness tell me she'd pop it in the bathroom or on my bedside table. Whenever her brother Peter-pink-car visited, he'd tease me: 'Doesn't Mama give you enough to eat?' (and my little hands would curl into themselves more tightly still). Once, my piano teacher told me if I stopped biting my nails then she would shout me a manicure as a reward. I acted grateful, and optimistic, but nothing changed. I could see how each lesson she'd notice my fingers, and look at them in the same resigned way I did: with a mix of dismay and disgust.

I don't know what my resistance to kicking the habit was. I know now that I probably couldn't have stopped even if I had tried, but stubborn child that I was, I think part of it was a deliberate (though secret) refusal to listen to my mother. It was the same thing with my refusal, right up until I left home at eighteen, to learn how to use a knife and fork. The more Mama chastised me, or made an example of my younger-by-five-years sister, the more fiercely I refused to give in. I guess I was attempting to assert my independence from my mother, who I was otherwise very used to appeasing. The deeper I dug in my heels, the higher the stakes felt, and thus the more humiliating the prospect of my defeat. I grew expert at using my fork to eat foods – chicken breast, sausages – that should have been cut, and silently prayed for meals like cauliflower cheese, fish fingers and spaghetti bolognaise. The occasional sight of a piece of veal or steak summoned in me a mild panic that I grew expert at masking. Papa colluded. He'd tell us, boastfully, how once his own father had criticised something about his table manners, and in response he'd cut a length of baguette, smothered it in jam, topped it with sardines, dunked it into his coffee, and then shoved it in his mouth, just to show his father that he would eat the way he liked. And if we had roast chicken, he'd always tell us – in that typical way fathers had, pre-internet, of being the font of all facts – how in fancy restaurants it was actually considered polite to use your fingers to eat chicken. Before Mama had the chance to intervene, I had only to slide my plate across to him and he'd obligingly cut up whatever it was with his wooden-handled Opinel pocket knife. Apart from his walls of books, my father was a man of few possessions. The knife, though, he took unguarded pride in keeping sharp. Years later, I myself use the same model and when my father (exactly twice my age this year) makes the trip from outer-western Sydney to my inner-western apartment, the first thing he'll do is sharpen it on the balcony using a brick. I've come to think of its sharpness or bluntness as a barometer for how recently he's come to visit.

Looking back now, to the turn of the century, I suspect my mother's jibes were the best way she knew to try to prod me out of my bad habits. I don't know whether at some level she was embarrassed that she should have a daughter with bitten nails, who couldn't even use a knife and fork. Or maybe just baffled, that her straight-A daughter, preternaturally disciplined in every other regard, should struggle with things so rudimentary. Maybe she detected my defiance, and was scrambling to stem it. Was she injured that I should injure the blossoming body that she herself had formed? My mother always told me that I had a good figure, and nice legs, and looked naturally pretty without needing any makeup. But in my fingertips lay our battlefield.

The weird thing was, she herself chewed her nails, though they were never half as bad as mine. My mother's hands were presentable, I guess you could say. Ever since leaving school at fifteen, she'd had the kind of jobs – factory jobs, nursery-hand work, fruit-picking – where it wasn't what your hands looked like that mattered, but how quickly and deftly they carried out the task.

She met my French backpacking father in far North Queensland in the eighties, picking tomatoes. They spent the following fifteen years making their living together in orchards across rural Australia (and, for a time, France, where my mother fell pregnant with me at twenty-four). The three of us, and eventually four, lived in a tent, and later a caravan, moving from farm to farm according to the seasons.

Sprawling fruit trees are the constant backdrop to my earliest of memories – I spent so much time among them that I came to know their cycles and their anatomy intimately. While my parents laboured I would draw endless pictures, and read my books, and make little mud-cakes. I mustn't have ever been more than fifty metres away from my parents, and every so often I might wander over to 'help' or to check how long it was until 'smoko', but essentially I was left alone, and I suppose it was in these early years that my propensity for solitude took seed.

I knew the exact consistency of the soil, just how much water needed to be added to form something pliable, the texture such that if you looked closely enough you could see the lines of my palm imprinted there. And I remember, in those years, how my mother's body bore the traces of her work: indentations between her shoulders and collarbones from where the wide straps of her fruit-picking bag used to sit, weighed down with some twenty kilos of oranges, and the same kinds of marks just below her knees, from balancing against the rungs of her enormous ladder, necessary to reach the higher fruit.

I remember my parents' frustration when other people – city people – would attempt to romanticise the work they did. The summers out west were inescapably hot (I was forever being warned not to touch the poles of our tent, or the metal clasp of my seatbelt, because they would burn to touch). The days were long, required great physical and mental fitness and endurance. But my parents, with quiet dignity, found great satisfaction in earning their living in this way. In an email to me not so long ago, my father described the satisfaction of the work thus: 'I remember being in a kind of trance, completely detached from the task itself.'

My parents didn't think our itinerant lifestyle would be compatible with my schooling, and so ended up settling on Sydney's outskirts, where they were employed on citrus orchards. On Saturdays, and in school holidays, in the very early mornings Papa would lift me, sleeping, from my bed, cradle me carefully in his arms, my head heavy against his shoulder, and carry me out into the bed that my mother would have made up in the back of our Kombi. He'd do the same with E's smaller body, and then a few hours later the two of us would wake in the orchard.

Every so often, mid-work, one of my parents would sing out to us: *a nest!* We'd climb our way carefully up to the top of the ladder, just to see the eggs, immaculate. Or sometimes even better: a clutch of naked babies, all skin and beak.

My mother was forever saying that if she were given the choice, she'd either want to live in the inner city, or else somewhere way out in the sticks, but not in-between. But in-between was where we were. She'd fantasise about one day buying a new Kombi, one that wasn't breaking down all the time, and returning to life on the road. 'I'd go back to living in a tent tomorrow,' she'd say, when the house piled with clutter became too much. For all its difficulty, our life in the tent had been a sort of elemental existence, which our move to suburbia quashed.

My mother wasn't the kind of woman who ever in her whole life set foot in a nail salon, or got her hair styled, or coloured. For most of my life she's kept her hair short, and now, she has let it naturally grey.

'It's *vulgar*, that's what it is,' she'd say about other women, who spent money on making their nails or their hair look nice. Both my parents had been raised in large, Catholic families and attended Catholic schools. One of my father's brothers became a monk, and one of my mother's sisters almost joined a convent, but neither of my parents were practising: they married after E and I were on the scene; they didn't get us baptised; as a family we never went to church. And yet, they still carried with them a view that pride and pleasure and personal vanity were, if not exactly sinful, nevertheless suspect. After all, and as I myself have come to understand, any lesson imbibed in childhood is not so straightforwardly shed.

As she's aged, my mother's hands have grown arthritic, her knuckles knobbly and painful. Her six-decade-old hands are a mother's hands: they are the hands that scrubbed and brushed and carried and chopped and sliced and sewed, and the most luxurious thing I've ever seen them touch is a tub of sorbolene cream. She has her Latvian father's fair skin and pale blue eyes, her Australian mother's thick dark hair, full cheeks, kind-hearted face, and tendency to slip into an expression of being ... somewhere else. Her body is a mother's body: wide hips, pouched stomach, heavy breasts. Apart from her underwear and her orthopaedic shoes, she only ever shops at op-shops (a habit my sister and I have both adopted). Nothing polyester: in summer, straw hats and cotton floral dresses, and in winter, woollen cardigans in neutral tones.

As far as I know my father has never bitten his nails; he's always kept them trim and neat. His hands are large and functional, the kind of masculine hands that have trouble threading a needle or pressing the buttons on a phone. By day, they were used to getting scratched and dirty. In the evenings, after he'd cleaned them with a plastic scrubbing brush and soap (that kind with grit through it), they were the hands that would grip my or my sister's ankles as he swung us upside-down, or let us try to balance upright on his shoulders.

He is at ease in his olive skin and in his slim, athletic body. Well into his forties, any patch of lawn was a chance for him to practise walking on his hands; any metal railing a chance to swing upside down. I knew, when I was little, that I had begun in Mama's tummy, but out in the world it was my father's body E and I were always clambering over. His chest we'd take turns sitting astride, prodding and pulling at his face, his beard. His stomach he'd get us to practise punching as hard as we were able, to prove to us that no matter how hard we hit, we could never hurt him.

Over the years, my nail-biting habit hasn't subsided. If anything, it's just gotten more intricate and more idiosyncratic. Since I started writing all this down in 2021, I've been paying closer attention to all the strange little rituals that I've incrementally developed, and which have become second nature to me. When I strip off another whisker-thin section of fingernail, for example, my habit is to lay it on my thigh. If there are several pieces then I will arrange them to lay across one another, like kindling. And then, whatever it is I'm doing, my eyes will keep on darting back to that particular location. Sometimes, inadvertently, I'll destroy the arrangement with a brush of my hand and then – protectively almost – I'll rearrange the careful structure. And if one nail fragment separates from the group then I'll nudge it back into its original position. If I have to get up to go to the bathroom or to make some tea then I'll deposit the little midden on my desk while I'm gone, and reassemble it on my leg when I return. Other times, if I draw blood, then the impulse is to press my finger like a stamp onto paper repeatedly. The effect is a series of one-winged butterfly prints like children make, or a kind of Rorschach test that nobody will ever take.

Another thing I do is use lead pencil to shade in the

entirety of (what remains of) my nails, which takes no time at all. I'll use the nib of the pencil to push back the cuticle far as it can go, so as to get the maximum surface area as I can, figuring, I suppose, that if I'm incapable of growing my nails in one direction then I may as well try enlarging them in the other. Then I squint my eyes so that I can just make out the dark shapes, inspecting and scrutinising them like a painter might do when she steps back from her easel. Sometimes, I'll bunch up four fingers and run my thumb back and forth along the nails' top edges, a repetitive gesture that's not unlike the one M makes when handling his prayer beads. ('Boyfriend' seems an inadequate word for M, my decade-long companion and confidant, but then, I find that's the case with so many words, and so for the time being, I suppose it will have to do.)

I find myself staring at my nails at every possible opportunity – when I turn the page of a book, my gaze darts to them (or sometimes it's between paragraphs), a constant shuttling of attention. Staring at my fingers as intently as I do, occasionally people have asked what I'm looking at, or offered a 'penny for your thoughts'. The truth is my whole attention is just going into tracing my gaze back and forth along the top ridgeline of nail, sometimes mentally calculating how many times the remnant of nail would fit into the space above it if it were multiplied (a good eight times, currently, for my ring finger). That's it, over and over again, tracing. When my nails are short as can be, other people – normal-fingered ones, I mean – must gawk at what is not there; what ought to be there; what has been removed.

But my own eyes only look to see what more can be taken; whether a nail is ready yet for another nick to be made, another crescent-strip to be peeled away.

The other day I left the house with a newly-obtained, sickle-shaped piece of thumbnail clamped between my fingers. I realised I must have been gripping it the whole time I was packing my backpack, putting my mask on, putting the rubbish out, checking the neighbour's recycling bins for bottles to take to the depot for my ten-cent refunds. Out on the footpath I held it out in front of me, taking in its unusual width – a good two millimetres thick, I reckon – and letting the sunlight shine its way right through it, surprised that my fingers could produce something of such size.

To this day I can't help – covertly – checking people's hands when I meet them for the first time, and I'm able to summon images of people's hands as clearly as I can their faces. What is it I'm checking for? Maybe for recognition, which I've almost never found. The only people I've seen who had nails like mine were on my high-school bus, which used to stop at some kind of centre for people with intellectual disabilities, to pick them up so they could go on excursions. Though recently I did meet Ursula – who according to her creator (D.H. Lawrence) 'had a cruel consciousness in her fingertips' just like me; 'a shame, an exposure' that haunted her beyond all proportion. 'She spent hours of torture, conjuring how she might keep her gloves on: if she might say her hands were scalded, if she might seem to forget to take off her gloves.' It was one of many moments in Lawrence that startled me, that this man who died half a century before I entered the world should know me and my fingers so intimately. I also half-wished I lived in an age where women still wore gloves.

Nobody really ever comments on my nails. But that doesn't mean they don't notice. And I'm alert to that moment, when they do – I can see plainly that they find my nails scary. Not scary like those SCARY NAILS? signs you see outside chemists with enormous photos of nails yellowed with fungi and craggy as oyster shells. Mine are scary in a different way – because it's quite obvious that I'm the one responsible; that the damage is all my own doing. Once, a friend who I was travelling with mentioned I could use her nail clippers and file at any point if I needed. It shocked me, that I had managed to deceive her so long; that even though we'd lived together through uni, she still hadn't noticed. How could I tell her that this everyday instrument was wholly unfamiliar to me? That I had always just used my teeth?

A couple of years later, embarking on a (very short-lived) primary-teaching career, I did my prac in what they call a 'multi-categorical' class – such an ugly word, I know – which is where the students have each been diagnosed with a whole constellation of different disorders. One of the kids was 'non-verbal', which meant he might occasionally parrot something the teacher said, mimicking the intonation perfectly ('Eyes on your work Josh, time to focus') or from a music video ('A little bit of Rita's all I need'), but he would very rarely produce any language himself. The smallest thing – a missing Lego piece; an apple's quarters being not quite even – would be enough for him to bawl into his beanbag for a good half hour.

When he did utter words – any words – everyone, the other students included, would encourage him. Like you might a toddler, except this kid was twice the size of a toddler. Despite the fact that I'd been warned against any physical contact with these kids, it often felt necessary. Crossing the quadrangle each morning after assembly, I'd take Josh by the hand – otherwise, he'd fall behind the others and we'd have to go searching everywhere for him. One day, he took my hand in his, inspected it, looked up at me, and asked simply, the concern in his voice unmistakable: 'What happened?'

My skin is the colour white children like to call 'skin-colour'; in other words it is the colour of bandaids. Which is lucky for me, because these days I have to remember to wear bandaids over my fingers as much as I can, even in those rare interludes when I feel safe (by 'safe' I don't mean safe from attacking my fingernails, but safe from succumbing to other, stranger urges, which I will tell you about in due course). I try to think of them like seatbelts, try to make putting them on automatic. The trouble is sometimes I forget I've got them on, but before anyone has the chance to notice or ask anything I surreptitiously strip them in my lap, scrunch them up, and ferret them away into the pockets of my coat (or sometimes down the side of a lounge) together with a collection of others. When I keep the bandaids on for too long and then take them off, the skin underneath is white and crinkled, like when my sister and I would stay in the bath too long and end up with what we used to call 'Chinese fingers'.

*

'Waste' was a dirty word in our family growing up. I don't mean dirty like oozy or putrid or something that belongs in the bin. To waste something was to be careless and ungrateful and undeserving. At the dinner table my father would dutifully scrape my and my sister's leftovers onto his plate. When I made cakes, my mother couldn't help checking the cracked eggshells, and if I'd left too much white behind she'd make sure I scraped it out properly with my finger.

To this day under her bed are garbage bags stuffed full of old clothes; the tops of her cupboards are lined with old glass bottles. So many things we've had so long that it seems a shame to throw them out now. She has held onto the tiny cardigans she knitted us as babies, to our childish drawings, our schoolbooks. Even to our milk teeth. (My teeth now are straight thanks to years of braces, but still just as sensitive as they've always been. I've never been able to bite into ice-cream, and I only ever drink water at room temperature, and this, along with all my other sensitivities, I have always considered a weakness. So much so that when not long ago my dentist did a 'cold test' and despite my efforts not to I flinched and she declared it a 'good sign', I didn't understand. 'Well it's good when you can *feel*,' she laughed, 'otherwise it might mean the tooth is dead.')

I don't know if she has it still, but in a small biscuit tin my mother used to keep a lock of my hair: so soft, and so fair, from the years before it curled, and coarsened, and darkened.

I have fought hard against my mother's hoarding tendencies, but I have always hoarded secrets. And so though telling this story feels like a betrayal, I would also like to see it as a heeding of her advice: for me to do nothing with all this silence and all this story – which is in part her story, too – would feel very much a waste.

# BEGINNINGS

My father had this habit, as he read, of touching his hair, which back in his forties was still black and curly. In my childhood drawings of him, his hair would loop around itself like an old telephone cord. As he read, he'd flick at a section of it, the kind of swiping movement you might make if an insect settled on your head, or if you were trying to remove some crumbs that had landed there. An unconscious thing no doubt. A sign of his absorption; his trademark position.

It was this flicking gesture that my mother would make, if ever she wanted to imitate him.

If ever we went to visit someone, the first thing my father would do would be to check their bookshelves. If they weren't well-stocked he'd consider this a travesty; a sure sign of mental poverty. I don't think it occurred to him that the mind might be occupied in other ways. My father reads like I've never seen anyone read. It is his habit to read novels in multiple translations, so he'd often have lain out in front of him the original version, alongside several others (sometimes he'd even compare different translations in the one language). His favourites are Proust, Zola, Flaubert. But he would read whatever he could get his hands on. At Coles, we'd lose him, and then find him, aisles behind, studying the labels of canned tomatoes or breakfast cereal. Sometimes he would buy things according to the array of languages the ingredients were listed in – he loved Pringles for this reason. On birthdays and Father's Days, when we each handed over a book-shaped object, he'd always make the same dad-joke, feeling it, and guessing: 'a bottle of wine? a pair of socks?' If we ever did choose him something that wasn't a book, he'd act pleased but later on say we could have bought a book for the same price – this wasn't done bitterly, more a gentle corrective for the future.

Whenever she'd get fed up with him – most often for always having his head in books – my mother would make a scene of dumping his Collins French dictionary in the garbage bin at the end of the yard, and then he'd make a scene of having to fish it back out, checking it tenderly to see it wasn't too damaged.

My father loves words. I don't just mean that he likes doing crosswords – it is far more specific than that. He treasures *individual* words and their etymologies in the same way that my sister is knowledgeable about the individual characteristics and provenances of the crystals in the shop she works. Take any word, and I really do mean just about *any* word, and he will be able to chart its journey through the centuries and into its present-day form. His auto-didacticism must have begun very early on: he remembers reading the dictionary as a child, cover to cover, as eagerly as though it were a Tintin comic, and I remember on our visits to France, his siblings, in that teasing imitating way that siblings do, would hold up items – a fork, say – and declare: 'Now, do you know the word for fork in Russian? And what about in Finnish? And did you know that in Hebrew ...'

Much of his contribution to conversation is a kind of linguistic free association. This has become utterly unremarkable to me, as is the case for so many unusual facets of those people we have known forever. Once, when my sister and I went for a visit after months in lockdown, over our coffee and croissants, E mentioned an importation to her shop of lapis lazuli from Afghanistan, apparently the only source in the world.

'You remember what lapis means in Latin?' my father interrupted my sister.

'Ummm ... stone?'

He smiled at her: 'Yes, like for "lapidary". And then lazuli ... what word can you see inside lazuli?'

'Laz, az ... azure!'

'Yes, the word for blue is actually similar in quite a few languages: in Spanish, *azul*; in Italian, *azzurro*.'

'Did you want me to heat up some more?' asks my mother, looking at our plates covered in flaky crumbs.

'Pourquoi pas,' answers my father. 'And what about croissant?'

'Crescent?'

'Yes, actually the shape was used to mark the defeat

against the Ottomans – you know how a lot of Arabic flags still have a crescent? And do you remember the trick I taught you, how to know if the moon is waxing or waning?'

E has forgotten but I remember, and so I remind her while my father listens:

'So if it makes a C shape, then you just remember *croissant* which means, "increasing" so obviously that's when the moon's getting fatter, and when it's more like a D shape, then you remember *de-croissant*: decreasing, so that's when it's waning.'

Mama is much harder to write about – harder to picture, even. I don't have any memories of her sitting – she was always *doing* something: checking on the potatoes in the oven, bringing in armfuls of washing, searching frantically for some misplaced item amid the clutter. (Visiting a friend's house once, and seeing his mother reading the *Herald* with her feet up on the sofa, I remember my bodily shock.)

I remember her specific ways of bringing us up, so wholesome. Brown rice; wholemeal bread; ABC TV. When we had coughs, she'd make us warm drinks of honey and lemon. Toothaches, a whole clove tucked in against the gum. For stomach aches she'd grate a green apple and spread it out evenly on a plate, and then we had to wait for it to turn brown before we ate it with a spoon. It was she who would always check we had enough blankets, enough suncream on, enough fruit for our school lunches.

Whenever I did something helpful she'd say: 'You'll

make someone a lovely wife one day' and whenever I found something especially good quality in an op-shop that wasn't yet my size, she'd say I should add it to my 'glory box'. These things she said with obvious irony, though I suspect her own mother, born in 1933, must have said these same words and meant them literally.

My mother's mother, Enid, came from humble Irish-Australian origins. In her day, she was a beauty; people used to say she looked just like Elizabeth Taylor. As was common for the time, she and my grandfather first met at a dance. Jāzeps (Joseph, or 'Joe' to Australian tongues) had been displaced from his homeland, Latvia, post WWII, and had come to Australia by ship. My grandmother would laugh about how back when they were courting, they'd arrange to meet at the beach, and he'd turn up in a full suit and tie, carrying a leather briefcase filled with salamis. He made his living here in Sydney as a railway guard; she kept house and raised their five children, on top of working part-time cleaning jobs.

I have good memories of our visits to Urunga, the North Coast town where they retired, 'where the rivers meet the sea'. My sister and I would hang out with Grandpa in his shed under the house, as he pottered away or re-did old furniture, an old transistor radio in the background, offering us bites of the whole raw onions he used to snack on ('very healthy' he'd coax us). With Nana, we'd go to play housie at the bowlo, or to the local Vinnies where she volunteered, or sometimes fishing with hand-lines for whiting, flathead and bream, which we invariably released, on account of E's sensitivity toward animals of all kinds. If I think of E back then, the image that comes to mind is of her tending to the little graves of mice, grasshoppers and pigeons (all cat-prey) in what she used to call her 'pet cemetery', or else high in the arms of the jacaranda out front, with one cat or another for company.

If the way my grandparents interacted with one another or the way they behaved at the dinner table was peculiar, as a child I must have put it down to their having grown up 'in the olden days', though when I do the calculations now, I see that in 1986, the year of my birth, my grandmother was only 53. She would fuss excessively over the dinner, and then once everyone had started eating, she was always checking if so-and-so wanted mustard, if anyone needed more salt, whether the water in the jug had enough ice, getting up unnecessarily and fiddling with things in the kitchen, putting barely anything on her own plate. Grandpa sat at the head of the table, and while we kids had been trained to pass things around in the one direction, and not to begin before everyone was seated and served, as soon as he sat down, he'd snatch at things from the centre of the table, and wolf them down like a man starving. (My uncle Peter-pink-car believes this habit must have originated in wartime, when he was, quite literally, starving.) Aside from her fretting, my grandmother would often tune out of whatever conversation was happening, getting that spacey look that usually only falls over the very elderly. At unexpected moments, my grandfather would enter the conversation to share a piece of Russian history or politics.

I can't say if, as a younger couple, their dynamic was different. I can't recall them ever touching one another, nor even exchanging any words. There was only my grandmother's high-pitched nagging at my grandfather (who never lifted a finger around the house) and his huffing sounds, both sounds that, as grandchildren, we used to find comical.

My grandmother, for as far back as my memory permits, appeared physically burdened. She was overweight, she had two knee replacements, and was forever apologising for not being able to walk faster, and only really able to shuffle along. She was – like so many women of her generation – the sort of person that others would describe as 'selfless'. She didn't like anyone to tend to her, always insisting she was fine, despite her many physical ailments. Her ring finger had fattened around her wedding ring; the ring was like a too-tight elastic band that could not be removed, and it stayed that way for years until my mother insisted on organising someone to saw it off.

My grandmother was generous to a fault: 'Did you see anything you liked?' she'd ask as we were leaving a shop. My grandfather would keep Mars Bars in the pockets of his pants, and smuggle them to me and my cousins when our parents weren't watching.

'They were *never* like that with us,' my mother would observe, wistfully, when she saw how they doted on their grandchildren.

I suspect that she means their affection and their warmth, but I haven't ever heard her use these words. When she does talk about what she lacked as a child, it is the tangible world not the emotional one that she speaks of. There were never books in the house (apart from some old copy of *Little*

*Women*). She never got to learn the piano, which she so would have liked. She therefore tried her best to provide my sister and me what she herself had lacked, reading to us from when we were babies, and taking us to the library nearly every weekend (she wasn't a big reader, and so it impresses me, now, to think that she should have recognised the importance of story), and organising weekly piano lessons.

At the same time as the lion's share of the housework fell on my mother's shoulders, she tried to instil a feminist consciousness in us, forbidding Barbie dolls and saying she regretted ever beginning to shave her legs, that we needn't, that once you started then you had to keep doing it forever.

*Don't stay out there too much longer or the mozzies'll eat you alive. Finish your crusts, don't you want curly hair? Careful not to swallow the seeds, you'll end up with an apple tree sprouting in your tummy. Don't throw the seeds on the ground, imagine if everyone did that! Don't use hot water to fill the jug, the pipes've got lead in them. Sit up properly. Why are you carrying your bag like that – use both straps or when you're old you'll end up with a body like mine. Go and put your slippers on, I don't want you to end up with a body like mine.*

Did I know, as a child, that this watchfulness, this caution, these constant acts of care – this was all proof of her unbending love?

She scorned the kind of parents who fed their kids anything too processed or frozen or coloured. When my sister wanted devon for her lunches like all the other kids, my mum would screw up her face and tell her: 'They make that stuff out of *embryos*.' She didn't seem to trust the kind of people who bought play-dough or birthday cakes from the shops instead of making them from scratch, and my sister and I learned to echo her scorn. I remember there was an ad on telly for a while where the kid pulls some homemade creation out of her lunchbox, proudly says how her mum made it, and then her friend whips out some packet thing and declares: '*My* mum's got a *life*.' How offended my mother used to get by that ad! 'The *hide* of it,' she'd say.

She couldn't believe parents who did things – any thing – without their children: parents who went out together for dinner, or hired babysitters. She'd shake her head and say she for one could 'never imagine' doing such a thing, as though it were some kind of abandonment.

All this will suggest to you that my mother was very present in my life. More than present: devoted. She was. Even now, after seventeen years living physically apart, so strongly does she loom in my psyche that when I do something careless, I conjure her caution; when I say something mean, I hear her dismay; when I make something nice, it is her approval I long for.

Within the midst of my childhood, though, despite my mother's physical presence, despite the fact we lived our lives alongside one another, despite our watchfulness of one another's movements, some part of her always felt absent and inaccessible. 'What's your favourite colour Mama? What about your favourite ... fruit?' I used to quiz her, and it was a family joke that she would always answer such questions with the same response: 'It depends.' When I hear scraps from other people it's nothing short of alarming, the idea that she might have other facets: a colleague of hers remarked that she has such a 'zany sense of humour'; when she was being treated for Stage III melanoma, her older sister remarked on the 'dignity' she seemed to possess. I've never been able to think of her as anything other than or larger than a mother; my mother. That goes for all children I suppose, but I feel it keenly still. As though her unknowability is in fact a fundamental part of who she is.

My father was born in 1951, just outside of Verdun, a town that had been practically destroyed in WWI, and then bombed heavily in WWII (a war in which his father had been enlisted at age fifteen). He was forever telling us about his own rough-and-tumble childhood, and as a result my mind is populated with stories involving goats and chickens; pigs and rabbits; snow-fights and fist-fights. He loved school. He used to get top grades for written assignments, though the teacher would deduct two marks for using pencil, not pen (pens were an expense his father could not afford). His teachers when they caned their students would make them hold their fingers pinched together and not flat-palmed, so as to sharpen the pain; his music teacher would 'correct' students' mistakes on the piano by slamming the lid down on their fingers. The neighbour's son used to get tied up with barbed wire by the other boys, snow smashed into his face. My father was spared this kind of routine bullying, thanks to the protection offered by his older brother, Noël: a fearless, street-smart boy who none of the other kids dared challenge.

What might today be considered hardship or poverty is

never framed as such by my father, who speaks of his childhood with an air of great hilarity and nostalgia. My mother, though, rarely spoke to us about her childhood, and when she did she would slip into a soft and rueful voice. She doesn't have good memories of her schooling, where she never really felt challenged. As a girl, she was expected to help out around the house in a way her brothers weren't. One of her brothers fell into trouble young. He'd get so ragingly drunk that the rest of the family would huddle on the hub of their little VW while he carried on inside the house, and my mother's youngest sister, terrified, would *shake* every time: this is the detail my mother emphasises whenever she speaks about it. When his ways became criminal, my mother threatened to dob him in to the police, but her mother insisted he'd 'just fallen in with the wrong crowd'. And it was her *daughter*, not her son, that my grandmother threatened to disown.

If this account seems to you riddled with holes, that is because it is. The origin of my uncle's alcoholism; the effect of this on the rest of the family; the circumstances of his death at age thirty-five; my grandparents' ensuing grief; a relative's chronic, lifelong mental illness; my grandfather's PTSD as a veteran; what it must have been like for my grandmother to be married to someone so emotionally detached and damaged ... none of these are questions I have the answers to, because there is an unspoken agreement in my mother's family not to ever mention or attempt to understand such things.

The one 'funny' story my mother tells is about Cracker Night (a tradition banned in NSW by the eighties). My mother collected a whole lot of ... fizzers, I think they're called?

and tied the wicks together to create a bigger explosion. The flame stopped partway, though, and so my mother bent down and blew hard to reignite it. It still didn't work, so she bent closer still, and this time the thing exploded in her face. Into the bathroom she ran, scrubbing desperately at her blackened face in the mirror, to remove the evidence, but instead the scrubbing only turned her skin raw. She realised she would have to face her mother; she was taken to hospital, where she had her entire head bandaged up, and was fortunate that her skin healed completely.

When I was a child listening to this story, what stood out to me was my mother's ingenuity, along with her daring: imagine doing such a thing behind everyone's back! What strikes me now is the impulse of that girl, who must have been in acute pain: not to run screaming to her mother, but instead, to hide. It is an impulse I have come to understand well. If my mother had been able to hide the damage she'd done, would she, all these years later, have told her daughters the story? Or would she have kept it secret forevermore?

And nor is much story told *about* my mother. She'd tell us what first attracted her to Papa: he used to walk down the street drinking two-litre cartons of custard; whenever they came across a cat he'd crouch down and talk to it tenderly, in French; he used to buy her totally unexpected and impractical gifts, like a Hungarian national costume. But I don't know what drew him to her.

The one story her older brother has kept alive through the years is of how once, at their Merrylands home, a neighbour's cat had kittens, and some strayed into their yard.

The little girl who would one day become my Mama wanted to reunite the babies with their mother, so she lobbed them carefully, one at a time, over the tall fence that divided their yard from the neighbour's. When my uncle tells this story it is with a jocularity: the things kids do! But each time he tells it, my mother looks humiliated, freshly wounded. Each time, she feels the need to explain herself again: 'I was only *little*. I didn't mean to *hurt* them.'

It makes me profoundly sad now that I have never heard her refer to *anyone* as a friend (if kids at school mentioned a friend of their mum's or dad's, it took me aback. I assumed friendship, like Lego or dolls, was the privilege of children). I have nearly no childhood memory of her doing something for the fun of it. Now, as an adult, I am filled with a kind of anger, at suburbia – at its capacity to isolate, its sterility – but at the time what I now recognise as frustration I saw only as her failing.

Now, when she picks up her landline, in that tiny window of time in which she does not yet know it is me who is calling, I savour her 'Hello ... ?' And what I hear is a small voice; it is a voice in need of reassurance.

My father's alarm would go off early, he'd mix together an ice-cream container's worth of muesli, rolled oats, Nescafé, Weet-Bix, sugar and milk, make himself some sandwiches of hunks of cheese and butter and salami and jam. He'd put on the boots that he'd have rubbed with Dubbin the night before (the waxy-tallowy smell reminds me of him still) and leave before the sun rose. ('Such a *martyr*,' my mother used to chide him, for the long and hot hours he would work.) At the end of days I would listen out for the distinct thrum of diesel, a sound that to this day I find deeply comforting.

My father's departure from our house and his return to it was marked, as is the case for so many a father. It was normal for him to have a place in the world.

My mother also worked full-time, but I have no memory of her leaving the house or of arriving. How is that possible? 'I'm like the invisible woman around here,' she used to complain and now I want to slap my child self, who wished only for her to stop whingeing.

Another thing I remember her saying, whenever she was at her wits' end: 'What did I *do*, to deserve *this*?' I remember countless times, asking her what was wrong, when she looked particularly upset or preoccupied or just sad ... and always the same response: 'What are you talking about? It's just my *face*.'

(And once I'd moved out of home, and would come back to visit, she'd sometimes look at my face, and say 'What's wrong? We're not going to play happy families just because you're here', as though this was more authentic, which I guess in a way it was?)

I remember countless times, when she got overwhelmed, asking her as politely as I could what needed doing, if there was something I could do to help, and then I'd be met with her laughter. A laughter without any happiness in it. The times I do remember her laughing – laughing properly – were watching TV: *Kath & Kim*; *The Vicar of Dibley*. I remember being resentful that these fictional characters could hold her attention and spark her laughter in a way that I couldn't, or had given up trying to. But also thankful, that for a window of time she was occupied, and her always-simmering anger was less likely to erupt.

I can't recall, now, precisely what it was that triggered these eruptions; it always seemed quite trivial, arbitrary things. I do recall, though, being acutely attuned to the preceding rumblings: she would get visibly flummoxed, start muttering to herself, repetitively questioning nobody in particular, and batting away any of our attempts to reply. Despite how obvious these signs were to me, she had little apparent awareness of her own escalating overwhelm. Inevitably, the explosion: banging of objects, unrelenting tears, and yelling that would last hours into the night ... she was never physically violent, but it was nevertheless terrifying to me: any attempt to reach her was entirely fruitless.

'You two are the only reason I stay with him,' my mother used to tell me, when my father was at work, and she was, yet again, seething with fury at him (there was her ongoing complaint that he should find a better-paid and more stimulating job; but more often there were his little infringements that she fixated on: his muddy boot-prints on the carpet by the door; his having put some kitchen implement on the wrong shelf; his wearing the wrong pair of socks; the volume of his early morning alarm, which prevented her from returning to sleep ... ).

I'm not sure the message she expected me to take from this refrain. That she despised him? Or that she loved us? That love was bound up in suffering and sacrifice? Or was she simply confiding her pain in me, because she had no-one else? The message I did take was that I was – if not fully, at least partly – responsible for her suffering. Any wonder then that I became such a 'good' and dutiful and helpful child? For which child wants to inflict pain on a mother already hurt?

Very occasionally – maybe annually, in the aftermath of Christmas – after an especially chaotic spell, she would reach out to hug me, tearily apologising for being 'so angry all the time', and I treasured these flashes of insight, my head held tight against her bosom. (Apart from our quick pecks goodnight, these were the only moments either of us initiated touch.) Usually, though, if I attempted to express how hurt I was by her explosions, and her volatility, she'd snap back 'it's not healthy to bottle everything up'. I chose to ignore this wisdom, and from a very young age, vowed that unlike her, I would keep everything *in*.

Perhaps you may be wondering where my father was in all this.

I don't know whether he ever stopped to ask himself if something was not quite *right* with my mother (or, for that matter, with her circumstances), or what impact her tempestuous moods might have on two young girls, especially ones as sensitive as my sister and me.

My father has a rare and wonderful quality to accept people and situations as they are. He considers his life 'blessed'; he says it makes no difference to him where in the world he lives, or what the landscape looks like: he is always in the same place anyway, which is in his head. If there is a dark side to this attitude, then it is a passivity: for my father, the world is the way it is; bloody conflict and suffering and violence have been constant through human history, and are an inevitable part of our present. People are the way they are; families, too; marriages, too.

He belongs to an age where the traits of a person – restless or aggressive or melancholy or alcoholic – are not to be pathologised or addressed, but simply facets of the self. (He remembers his own father as 'kind of frail, and very very sad'.) And so I suspect that even if, at some level, he *was* aware that my mother seemed prone to worry, and had a short temper, and misplaced things easily, and withdrew in conversation, and saw a delayed train or a lost umbrella or unapplied suncream as cause for panic, this was just who she was, as beyond our influence as the weather.

I don't know whether a different sort of husband might have been less accommodating of – or at least less oblivious to – my mother's extremities; might have been better equipped to *do* something.

When my uncle visited (just about the only guest we ever had), I remember my father would say casually to me beforehand: 'It'll be good, for Mama to have a break from yelling', because this was another unspoken rule: that in the presence of a guest we would act like a 'normal' family. I remember on more than one occasion one or another of my mother's siblings visiting the house and, despite my parents' concerted efforts to tone things down, as soon as my mother was out of earshot one of them would tell my father: 'You shouldn't let her speak to you like that.'

And each time, his bemused laughter: 'She can talk to me however she likes. She's my *wife*.'

In some ways – important ways, which I don't want to downplay – our family life was highly functional. We ate our dinner together every night. My sister and I got taken to music lessons and sports lessons and orthodontist appointments and birthday parties. On weekends, we'd go on long bushwalks as a family, or for swims at the local pool.

My parents valued our education highly. My mother, especially, nurtured our creative pursuits – music, drawing, painting, story-writing – and she never put pressure on us to achieve certain marks in the way I knew some other parents did. I always found it hard to buy presents for her (books would go unread; jewellery would get lost) but the one thing she reliably liked, and likes still, is anything handmade by me or my sister: watercolour paintings; collages; ceramics ... I remember how from when we were very young she would handle these objects with such reverence, and say, almost shyly: 'You could be an *artist*', which we took as the highest of possible compliments.

For his part, my father would read every reference book we borrowed for school projects, no matter how obscure the subject matter, just so he could discuss the topic with us. We were surrounded by books: children's encyclopaedias; Agatha Christie novels; guides to magic tricks and spy-craft; books to identify native birds and plant species; myths and legends and folktales; recipe books and atlases and travel guides from around the planet. My father would quiz us on the capital cities of the world ('Honduras?' 'Belize?'); the collective names for different animals ('owls?' 'bats?'); the names for baby animals ('baby swan?' 'baby hare?') and we all seemed to agree that this kind of knowledge was important. But when it came to emotional territory our vocabulary was restricted.

'How are you going?'/ 'How are you feeling?' are phrases I can't ever remember hearing in our family. Nor: 'I'm sorry'. Nor: 'Thank you'. Nor: 'I miss you'. Nor: 'I love you'. We used to joke that we'd heard about families who held weekly meetings or 'conferences' to discuss things. How bizarre! How embarrassing! Now, I wonder what might have become of my girl-self, had she been given a space where things – life – could be talked through, calmly and safely.

I remember this one time, my mother was switching over medications of some kind (for hay fever or arthritis or high blood pressure – I can't recall), and this was affecting her mood such that she had ended up losing her temper at work: how mortified she was about this crack in the smooth I of the self she presented to the world.

A memory keeps returning to me, of which my sister has no recollection whatsoever (erased, perhaps, by the amnesia which is said to interfere with toddler-minds). I don't remember now, where this place was or why we were there; it must have been a birthday celebration of some kind. I remember the chair by the backyard pool, a 'love-seat' my mother taught me – but I only remember that curious detail because of the sequence of events that unfolded next. Me swimming up the deep end, my sister maybe only five metres away at the shallow end, but in such a small pool the transition from standing on tiptoes to getting out of one's depth is not spaced out, like in a public pool, and so before anyone could foresee it, my sister panicked at not being able to reach the bottom. I remember her arms flailing, clinging to me, me gasping for dear life, and then being dragged under again, gasping again, and then newly dragged under, and my mother jumping in to rescue us, fully clothed, wrenching my sister off me. And everyone else there gathered on the edges, like it was a film they were watching.

When she related the incident to Papa later that evening it was her shoes she kept repeating, how lucky it was she'd kicked her shoes off before jumping in. There was one point where she didn't think she could make it, thought that maybe she should just 'let herself go'. This exchange between my parents was memorable not only for its gravity, but also for the fact it did not escalate into argument.

I don't know whether it began before or after that day of the pool, but my mother would announce from time to time that she thought drowning would be the best, the gentlest way to die. And then she'd add she wouldn't want to be buried, that she would want her body to be burnt. Which would prompt my dad to scoff at the waste of coffins and flowers for the dead, and to check we were clear about which song he wanted played at his funeral (Brel's 'J'arrive'). And then my sister and I – who had never fantasised about our weddings in the way of most girls – would start fantasising about our own preferred destiny, which was to be placed on a clifftop and eaten by ravens.

My mother struggled so frantically that day, under the weight of us, and who can say, now, how evident her struggle was to anyone else, or why nobody attempted to help. Now, it is hard for me not to see her floundering as metaphor.

'Don't tell Mama, though,' is a phrase my father, my sister, and I have always used with one another after we share something, however minor or however serious, that we know will trigger her worry or scold. As an adult, whenever I tell her not to worry about something, she will, reliably, respond: 'But I'm your *mother*.' It seems, for her, that motherhood is synonymous with concern.

Perhaps this assessment is unfair of me. Alongside her dominant mode of fretting, I know there is also pride, and love, and tenderness.

But these things, in our family, are seldom expressed.

When I'd do exceedingly well in school, other parents would tell my parents they must be so proud of me, and my dad would say, afterwards: 'Proud? Why would *I* be *proud*? Adele's the one who's done the work!' (Though to be fair, more than once in the past few years he's said to me or to E that he really can't imagine how he would have coped if he'd had kids who turned out 'stupid'. This, I think, is his roundabout way of telling us he is proud of who we've become.) Not long ago, Peter-pink-car recounted how when he said to Mama

— just after my HSC results came out — that she must be so proud of me, she retorted that he ought to see the state of my bedroom. Mama looked not just irritated but defensive, and she turned to me: 'I'm sure that wasn't the *first* thing I said.'

I can't say, now, how accurate my uncle's version of events is. To me, what's more important is my mother's obvious shame at this version of herself, which she, today, finds unrecognisable. And yet that is the version of her I know most intimately.

When you say 'mother' or 'father', writes Rebecca Solnit, you describe three different phenomena, and together they make up a 'chaotic and contradictory trinity'. 'There is the giant who made you and loomed over your early years; there is whatever more human-scale version might have been possible to perceive later and maybe even befriend; and there is the internalised version of the parent with whom you struggle — to appease, to escape, to be yourself, to understand and be understood by.' I don't know that I have ever managed to reduce my mother to human-scale. It is the internalised version of her that is with me, always.

And of course, however much I wrestle with these three versions of my mother, there is yet another still: the one who lives inside her; the one I know nothing about.

Once, when my sister and I were sifting through stuff in our grandparents' garage, we came across a sketchbook with our mother's name on the front. Her maiden name, the name that belonged to that mysterious time before our mother was a mother. Inside were drawings, drawings like I'd never seen before: fastidious mandala-like patterns, not dainty, but alien and alive and violently beautiful. I had never known my mother to draw (though when she was on the phone she used to doodle on scraps of paper, and these drawings too were elaborate and intricate). Whenever we mentioned this book to her, she'd brush it off: 'Oh yes, people did use to tell me I had a good eye.'

For a time, she worked in a factory manufacturing aerosols, paint mostly. She hated it; it was monotonous and suffocating, and she would come home headachy and stinking of chemicals, the kind that she herself would never use, and no matter how much she tried, she could never be entirely rid of the stench of the place. I remember her manager organised a Secret Santa, and she spent an entire evening baking shortbread, flavouring it with wattle seed she had ground herself, and then wrapping it carefully, trying out one ribbon and then another from the collection of assorted ribbons she had saved from birthdays and Christmases past.

How sad, that this was where her artistry went. I believe my mother contained great creative potential, a potential that the world mostly forced her to keep latent and never gave her the space to tap.

One of the clearest memories I have is of the time she got herself drunk on sherry. I think I was nine. She'd been so incredibly wound-up (I don't want to use the word 'hysterical') that Papa had hit her with a cricket-bat-sized length of wood, the kind that my sister always had lying around to construct mazes for her mice.

I remember her fury: 'No man should *ever* hit a woman.' And I remember us – to the deep shame of my present self – defending Papa, saying he'd only done it to try to make her calm down, and that made her more furious still, that we had taken his side. She disappeared into the kitchen and what I remember is when she returned, my sister sprang out of her armchair and rushed into my lap, clinging to me and screaming: it was our mother but it was not our mother. It was like someone else was in her body: she was calm, smiling, warm. 'Tu fais peur aux filles,' (you're scaring the girls) said Papa. In the kitchen, I remember that she was balancing a broom upright, swatting awkwardly at the high ceiling in an attempt, perhaps, to remove the cobwebs that collected there. I remember later, when it was our bedtime, she crowded into the bathroom with us and brushed her teeth the same time as us and instead of spitting, she spouted the water out of her mouth into the sink. I remember this because she was playful. And present. All of this is so vivid because it only happened once.

I'd never seen either of my parents drink enough to notice any shift in how they carried themselves. I was used to them having a half-glass each of cask wine with dinner, diluted with tap water. It would take them several weeks to get through a single cask of Kaiser Stuhl (I kept track because I liked to use the emptied foil bladder as a pillow). In fact, as a kid I'd probably never really seen anyone drunk. (Well, apart from my mother's younger brother, but back when he was alive, I was still young enough to be oblivious to the fact that he always had alcohol on his breath.)

Nor was my father a violent man. The knife he always carried on him, he'd turn blade-side up, hold his tongue outstretched with the other hand, catch our attention and then pretend to saw into it, my sister and I shrieking, my mother warning, 'One day you'll slice your tongue in half'. In his car he kept a mallet within arm's reach in case someone ever attacked him, though no one ever did. Sometimes my sister and I liked to copy every single thing he said, trying to echo his intonation between fits of giggles. Eventually he'd tell us we needed to stop: '(Ça suffit maintenant.' And we'd copy that, too, and then he'd raise his voice and tell us he was being serious now, but even when his 'anger' escalated we knew he wasn't *really* angry with us; it was the kind of pretend anger that kids can see straight through.

The memory of that evening has stayed with me precisely because it is so unusual:

My father never lost his temper.

My sister and I rarely touched one another.

And I can't recall my mother ever being calm.

It's impossible to say how much of any of this she remembers now; nor whether any of this was even formed into memory at the time. I remember as a teenager getting infuriated with my mother, that many a morning after an evening of screaming so badly she would lose her voice, she'd dismiss her outbursts, as though *I* were the one being ridiculous. As soon as her own emotion had dissipated, we were all expected to move on: no time to dwell on these things.

I have always found it so fascinating (and unfair, too) that our earliest years on this planet, when we are entirely dependent on our parents, should vanish from memory. If there is a consolation for parents, perhaps it is this: they alone determine how that stretch of time gets told.

I have often wondered, though, whether there is another kind of amnesia ... when strung-out parents, torn between different demands, throw plates of food, and upend furniture, and hiss vicious things, do they remember those things as clearly as their children do? Or do those things need to be forgotten?

Sometimes, when her own mother was 'flying off the handle' (as my mother's sister worded it) my mother would take me aside and whisper to me, the sensible eldest grandchild: 'Promise me you'll tell me, if ever I get *that* bad.'

As far back as I can remember, I saw my mother's volatility as something frightening, and my father's self-sufficiency and restraint as traits to emulate.

In my child-mind, my own propensity to tears I saw as something that required overcoming. And Papa's predictability and imperturbability were qualities that I considered not just desirable, but my true self, who I would be when I grew up. So if relatives pointed out that my hair was as thick as my mother's, or that she used to have cheeks as full as mine when she was a girl, I would pray that our resemblance was only skin-deep. Any comment my mother made that aligned me with Papa pleased me: my knees cracked when I bent down, just like his; I liked eating the skin off milk heated in the saucepan, just like him.

And when, at age seventeen, I started to play with my hair as I read, my mother would say, endearingly, that I was 'just like Papa'. She mistook it for his gesture, and this alignment with him was something I wanted to encourage, as well as a convenient cover for what it was that I was really doing.

Who of us could have known, then, that this gesture was anything but innocent?

Who could have foreseen that this domestic scene could be the backdrop for my unravelling?

# HAIR

I'd always kept my hair pulled back – wearing it down, especially just after I'd washed it, my hair was too dramatic, like I was making some kind of statement. 'American girls'd kill to have big hair like yours,' my mother used to tell me. I was not the kind of girl who wanted to draw unnecessary attention to herself, though, and especially not on account of my appearance. My hair had always been far too thick for my liking. I remember meeting one of our Latvian relatives for the first time, out the front of Blue Mountains Botanic Garden in Mt Tomah. When she embraced me, the first thing she did was pick up my plait in her fingers and hold it aloft, and even though we couldn't communicate I knew she was admiring its size. I must have been going on thirteen (in other words, well before my problems began). But I felt myself bristle, like a cat that doesn't want anyone touching her tail.

(My sister has much thinner hair, that is far more … manageable. As is typical for a girl, her style of dress changed every year or so, and her hair, too. At age fourteen she cut her own fringe in the mirror; at sixteen she began experimenting with red henna; at nineteen she shaved one side of her head, and then, a few years later buzz-cut her entire head, and this is how she keeps it now.)

I felt what can only be described as shame at how my hair looked undone (if only I knew, then, how profoundly this shame would grow) – it didn't work with gravity like other girls' hair; it took up too much space. Wet, it would take so long to dry that I'd have a towel around my neck for a good couple of hours afterward, so the back of my shirt wouldn't end up saturated. For school, I would bunch it up and fasten it to my scalp with bobby pins; I'd need at least a dozen to do the job, to make my hair take up as little space as possible. Other girls at school would have their hair done differently all the time (pigtails/French braids/half-up-half-down, different ribbons and butterfly clips), and there would be much cooing and comparing each morning. If a boy had got a number one – which was regarded as somehow edgy – the girls would caress his head like it was a kitten. My hair stayed the same, though. It was so used to being kept in its position that my scalp would ache if I tried to so much as part it differently.

My father was never fussed about appearances, but he had two nuggets of wisdom he liked to repeat about women: they looked better with long hair, and they looked best wearing skirts or dresses (in the 1950s rural working-class world of his childhood, a female schoolteacher of his who turned up in pants was viewed as shockingly radical). I admit that when he used to deliver this fatherly wisdom, it did not occur to me that Mama followed neither of these conventions.

The hair-related wisdom our mother imparted to us was strictly practical: *Don't rinse out all the conditioner; don't brush it while it's wet; don't go to bed with wet hair; don't rub at your hair like that, just let it dry. Use a scrunchie, that elastic's too tight. You have lovely hair, you don't need to* do *anything to it.*

Except for the occasion of my uncle's wedding, I'd almost never been to the hairdresser's (and, for reasons you will come to understand, have never stepped foot in such a place since). My mother was always the one to cut my hair, an event as routine and unceremonious as rubbing suncream on one another's backs at the pool. I'd wash my hair, then before it quite dried, take a chair into the yard, and wrap an old sheet around me. Mama would comb out my curtain of hair, and then trim a couple of centimetres off the ends as evenly as she could while I tried to keep my head still. We never had any layers, or experiments, though maybe once I had a fringe? I recall the small shock every time of tying my hair back in a ponytail once it dried, and even if only a centimetre had gone, the curious sensation of it ending too short, fingers snatching at air.

Even until I was an age where I should have been too old for such things, my mother would brush my hair each morning. I would stand with my back to her, pass her the brush (which always first needed to be found) and a scrunchie. We all used to use the same bathwater, and we shared the one brush, too – a smooth oval head and thick, wiry boar bristles. She would brush it straight, which I never liked, since unbrushed it would have a curl to it, but brushed it would just turn to frizz.

I could tell her mood by the way she brushed my hair. This suggests *that* was how I gauged her mood, but in actual fact I always knew her mood, could detect it in an instant. In her brushing, it was made physical: the knots being untangled, the bristles eating into my scalp. If I complained, then Papa would call out: 'Faut souffrir pour être belle' (one must suffer to be beautiful). I remember when he took us to France and in Mama's absence had to brush our hair. How different it felt – like he had no idea how much pressure to put, like he was swatting at our hair rather than brushing it. No doubt he was scared to hurt us.

I had never been one to pay too much attention to my hair, nor indeed to any part of my body, save my fingers. But in my HSC year, aged seventeen, as well as learning about the Ancient Greeks and the Victorians and the Post-Impressionists, I began to discover the anatomy of my hair. A lot of the ends were split, and tendrillous; I would peel the splits up, far as they would go before detaching from the main hair's shaft. And then I started to do this other thing, an arresting thing ...

Each individual hair I pulled out – curled and coarse – I'd stretch out tight, and take in the enormous length of each one unfurled. If I ran one along my thigh, it would reach from my hip to my knee. And how dark. I wasn't used to thinking of my hair as being that dark. All the bits on the outside were lightened by the sun, and sometimes, in the mirror, I'd hold different bits of it against one another, just to compare the colours – some bits redder, some slightly blonder. Sometimes the one hair gradated, a bit like a cat's brindles. But the hidden bits, I mean the bits that grew out from the central part of my scalp – they never got to see the sun, so they were almost black. The whole process was mysteriously painless: the hairs on my head, I learned quickly, sit as shallowly as birthday candles in a cake, can be removed as effortlessly as a grape can from its stem.

Before I go on, let me say that the chapters that follow this one may be hard for you to bear; unless you are of my kind, doing what I do would hurt you. And I would believe your hurt, I would, because occasionally when a hair of mine catches in the Velcro of my bike helmet, or when some of those tiny vellus hairs on my arm get stuck in the glue of a bandaid as I'm trying to coax it off, I can't help but release a tiny yelp.

Back in that HSC year I had so much hair, and it was all so thick that I (deludedly, I now realise) never contemplated the fact that by pulling out individual strands I was doing any damage. In fact, if anything, I thought I was tidying up my head of hair by thinning it out a little. Like a gardener might thin out seedlings, so that there aren't too many roots all vying for the same patch of earth.

Pulling out just one shaft of hair at a time always felt so insignificant, something imperceptible. Who could notice one strand missing from a whole, overly thick head of hair?

Once they'd been removed from my head I would stuff

the hairs away down the side of my bed. These discarded hairs held no interest for me. One day, I was cleaning my room – always a rare occasion as a teenager – once it had become a necessity, when all the surfaces had been completely covered in teacups containing liquids at various stages of decay, and all my clothes were in their third cycle of being worn. Anyway, I shoved my hand down the side of my bed, collected all the hairs I could and rubbed them together between my palms into something resembling a scratchy ball of wool. I kept on scraping up more hairs and adding them to the ball. I shoved the whole thing into a plastic bag, this object the size of a small bird's nest and when I went to double-bag it, so I could dispose of it in the garbage bin at the end of the driveway, what threw me was the weight of it. I never knew hair had weight. I can still feel the heft of it.

Maybe the word evidence is a strange one to use here. I wouldn't use it for the tiny, blunt hairs that stuck to the sides of the bathtub after I'd (secretly) shaved my legs, or for the small mounds that I'd seen carpet the floor of hairdressers in shopping arcades. But there was no doubt in my mind that *that* was what was contained in the plastic bag. Evidence. By this point in my life I'd already internalised the belief that the way I was always picking at my nails was ugly and unladylike (unhumanlike even), and this new habit seemed far more aberrant. Even picking parsley from the garden for dinner, my mother had taught me the 'right' way to pinch just the tips, not to pick too much from the one part of the plant, and certainly not to yank at it in such a way the roots might be dislodged. And so now, with my hair, there was no doubt whatsoever in my mind that what I had done was unspeakable, and wrong.

Once a week or so, I'd wash my hair. Dry, it was too massive, and felt unmanageable. But wet, it glistened itself into tightish curls, and took up a fraction as much space. Washing it was always such a task, because it knotted so easily. More than once I remember being brought to tears because I wasn't able to get the knots out, and my arm was tired from the sheer tugging. At some point I was washing it and I felt with my fingers right in the very centre of my head. After my shower, I took a mirror, held it over my head and then stood in front of the floor-length mirror behind my bedroom door and there it was: a patch about the size of a twenty-cent piece, perfectly clean. Not just thinned, but actually one hundred per cent bald. What was the feeling I had? Shock, certainly, but mixed in with it, a kind of satisfaction (same as when a bruise surfaces maybe). Now, I had two sets of evidence: one on my body, and one detached from it.

When he was a teenager, Tim Winton says that whenever he had the house to himself, he would go to the wardrobe, and remove his father's rifle (for his father was a policeman). 'I handled it soberly, with appropriate awe ... [I] knew I had the means of destruction close at hand ... It was such a charged and sneaky compulsion. I waited for any opportunity; anticipation was part of the thrill.'

Do all children-no-longer-quite-children require such private spaces to retreat to? I was a child who felt too much and who was afraid to express herself freely, afraid to take risks or make mistakes or be criticised – did I need somewhere unwatched and unmothered; a reprieve from the perpetual intrusion of my mother's moods; a place that nobody else could join? 'I was appalled by its atavistic potency, yet I was entirely in its thrall.' Or did I maybe just need, finally, the chance to do something *bad*?

I don't know if there was an exact point at which I realised I wasn't able to stop. It must have been somewhere between when I genuinely believed I was tidying my hair up and when it got to the stage where 'doing my hair' each morning (soon as I woke, before I got to the breakfast table) involved an elaborate and humiliating process – sweeping my fringe back to cover the top part of my scalp, drawing up the side wisps, and sweeping up the back and plastering it onto my head with bobby pins to keep the arrangement intact.

That point must have been in my eighteenth year, when I was still living at home, making the long daily commute into the city for my first year of university. I was nonconformist (or uncool) enough for people to assume I had especially chosen this hairstyle, however odd and unflattering it may have been. I was fortunate, too, that my mother and my sister were not the kind of women to engage in conversations about hair (the kind of conversation that I'd spend the next decade studiously evading). I made next to no friends at university, and was obsessively in love with my first-ever boyfriend, a mountains-boy who'd been in my (all-male) circle of friends in the latter part of high school, who made up secret alphabets in his spare time, and who was mercifully oblivious to such things as nail polish and bobby pins.

Over the next several months, unbeknownst to anyone around me, the patch grew, expanding until I had pulled out a good fifty per cent of my hair. These were the pre-Doctor Google days. We had a family computer, and a modem, but I only ever used them for assignments, and even then, made sure to avoid any sites with imagery (which would take too long to load). In any case, you need to understand that at the time, this was just something I did. It didn't occur to me that what was developing in my bedroom and in my fingertips had any connection to anything larger than my own precious secret world. It didn't cause me pain; even though I considered it 'wrong', it wasn't a great source of anxiety.

Here's the other thing: in the 90s, and in the early 2000s (at least in the outer suburbs where we lived) people didn't talk about mental health with any kind of openness. (A public health campaign on telly in those years, warning: 'One in five Australians will experience a mental illness in their lifetime' and each time, predictably, my dad would turn to each of us, pretending to need to count. Joke being: the fifth person – the crazy person – wasn't in the room.) In my final year of high school, we had a fundraiser for Beyond Blue, and were told the money would go towards mental illness and suicide prevention. This struck me as a worthy cause, but one as removed from my own world as though we'd been doing the 40 Hour Famine to raise money for unspecified 'people in Africa'.

Nowadays, people my age will mention 'my therapist' as openly as my parents might have said 'my mechanic' or 'my boss'. Somebody tidy will get described as 'a bit OCD', someone moody as 'bipolar'. Teachers, I've noticed, will take it upon themselves to diagnose fidgety kids as 'ADHD', dreamy ones as 'obviously on the spectrum'. ('Seems everyone wants to have their own little label,' my father likes to say.) That clinical terms are used so casually and so imprecisely can be frustrating. But at least the words have entered our vocabulary.

In any case, back in my late teens, I didn't have any sense that removing the hair from my head was anything other than a wholly physical act. The knowledge that my hair-pulling was in fact following an eerily predictable, pathological path wouldn't have fazed or interested me. This all felt, from the very beginning, that it was all my own doing, and I was, by that point, already too far gone.

# ANATOMY OF PULLING

This curious habit of mine is now in its seventeenth year, which is the same age I was when it began. It's hard for me to write about any of this. For a start, it has all become second nature to me. And also, it's hard to describe any of it without having hover over me the thought of the words being read. How your face will pucker, your eyes narrow, like you've bitten into something unripe, or discovered the source of a bad smell.

Implausible as it may sound to you, sometimes the urge to pull is a kind of zinging in my arms, a physical anticipation in the same way that the tongue salivates at the thought of food (and like hunger, such an urge can only be staved off for so long). Sometimes the need is like when you've been underwater as long as you can bear, and you can think only of one thing. Sometimes it's only a faint itch, though it is these lesser urges that can be the riskiest of all, since they trick you into thinking that this time you're in control, this time you have a handle on it.

Before I know it, my fingers are prowling for the right hair, and then they pounce. (I feel compelled to use present tense here. I have made these movements thousands upon thousands of times over, and they no longer feel attached to any one particular point in time, but belong to an eternal present.)

At different times, different ones call out to be pulled. The chosen hair should be thick as possible, and not too short, since I need to be able to get some purchase on it. About the length of a toothbrush's bristle.

Most people probably conceive of their hair collectively – as blond, or frizzy, or shoulder-length – whereas for me, my attention once I begin zooms in on a single hair. Before, I never thought about the hairs on my head as having individual characteristics, but they do. And it is this individuality I am on the lookout for. This might be a question of thickness – some kinked like old wire; some whisker-thin. And each time my hands flutter up to my scalp, despite having traversed it so many thousands of times, it never feels the same (in the way that the same beach can feel changed each time, according to the season, the tides, the light). Hair is anything but static: its quantity is always multiplying (or in my case fluctuating) and its texture is always changing, too, according to when it's last been washed, or brushed, and what kind of shampoo you used, and the humidity. The probing and stroking in itself can be enough to tease the hair, and so to alter how it feels.

The right hair is not only about texture or length, but also position. Those with the most magnetic pull are those at the crown of the head, the section of my hair that – if it existed – would be the centre of the whorl. If that area is too sparse, though, then the space directly behind my forehead's hairline is next in line, and if not there, then anywhere that orbits the centre will do. Too close to behind the ears hurts. The parts of my head that have been pulled from the most are much more appealing than those that have never been – I have been pulling so long now from these patches that the quality of the hair itself has changed.

You might imagine I would eventually run out of hairs to be pulled; that pulling as much as someone like me, you'd fast be left with total baldness. But even though the urges wax and wane quite dramatically – violently, even – I seem to have subconsciously tempered my habits so that I manage to pull at such a rate and in such a particular pattern that overall there is a basically even spread of hairs at each single stage. By which I mean: some sections of scalp will be near-bare; these are the freshly plucked follicles, which I have noticed seem to lie dormant longer than if the hair had been shaved, and when eventually the tip does emerge it is tapered. If there is a little cluster of these tapered hairs then this growth will appear feathery, like a dandelion gone to seed. Some sections will be stubble-length, by which point the hair starts to emerge noticeably coarser. At this stage the hair is not quite long enough to grasp. I couldn't tell you how many days before it reaches the graspable stage, since when it comes to these matters my only barometer is touch. Once the hairs are long enough for my fingers to have some purchase on them, this is when they are most likely to end up on my bathroom floor or in my lap. If individual hairs are sufficiently resisted and survive this precarious phase, and achieve some extra millimetres of length, then they become the most endangered-feeling of all, like they've somehow outlived their prognosis, like storm clouds heavy with rain, like the temptation of overripe berries to birds.

And so: even in the wake of a ravenous episode, still I trust that the next crop is on its way, will be here soon, like a gardener who's sown seeds in the winter and anticipates the shoots poking their tender tips above the earth's surface.

And another thing: there is no limit to how many times I can pull from the one spot. The supply is – as far as I know – as bottomless as rain, or tears.

I move between these different sections of my scalp like a farmer rotates livestock between paddocks. Sometimes one plot will lie fallow, until it's had time to grow and form a kind of springy thickety layer. This requires an enormous investment of time and willpower, but I know that, like a jackpot, the longer I am able to resist, the greater will be the rewards. I come to think of my scalp as a swathe of land that keeps on getting logged. Patchy, razed, and pitiful, and you can't help but be shocked by the damage, at how long those trees must have taken to reach that height, only to be uprooted. And how thick and dense and *alive* the original growth.

Around the very perimeter of this small territory are the only hairs that are safe, and that I manage to resist. This rim of hair is what, several times a day, gets gathered up and tied together in the centre, so as to veil the ravages that lie beneath it.

If you imagined my head as a globe, then this ring of

hair would form a circumference; roughly where a crown of thorns would sit, if for some reason I were to wear one.

And there is something else I almost forgot, so natural it has come to feel: that if, say, I pull from the right side of my head, then I (or should I say my fingers? I am not sure at this point who or what is in control) will need to pull from the left side in the corresponding location, as though my scalp had a line bisecting it (in the way that the brain is divided into two hemispheres) and that touching one side lit up the corresponding nerves on the opposite side, so that my hands shuttle from one side to the other like a tennis ball gets hit back and forth over a net. Most hairs won't make any sound as they get extracted; with some you can hear a tiny squeak.

At any single moment in all this, I am altogether fixated on one single hair, but actually my fingers seem to move from point to point on my scalp so deftly and with such surety that if someone were to see me from above (which is something that often occurs to me in these moments, what I would look like from above) they might think my fingers must be moving in accordance to some greater design, like a needleworker's, or like a spider darting from point to point to build her web.

How to capture any of it? How is it possible for a mind to occupy itself with something this narrow? And with such ferocity? The same thought over and over and over again, that never feels tired or old and has me entirely in its thrall: that I need to get *this* one.

It's a bit like collecting seashells, which I have always enjoyed more than being in the actual surf. I mean that there is no clear point at which to stop, because you never know what's coming, what else you might find. And when you find a good one, you get tempted to look close by for more.

My mother appreciates the surf more than I do. She likes stretches of proper, wild surf—rough and unpredictable, and turns her nose up at images of places like Jervis Bay, all white sand and so peaceful and boring. Two Christmases ago Mapa came to visit M and me at an Airbnb we were staying in on the Central Coast. 'Mapa' is how E and I now refer to the two of them, now that they are more of a unit. Especially so since 2012, when my mother fell very ill. A melanoma had spread to her lymph nodes; the surgery left her with permanent nerve damage between the knee and hip, and then in 2018 it recurred. Her immunotherapy treatment would leave her body aching, especially at night, but she found the pain eased with walking and with swimming.

Throughout her long sickness, she would email us appointment times and dates for scans, and links to podcasts and fundraisers ... but none of us ever really broached the topic of her fear, or her state of mind, or the question of her own mortality. I don't know if or how other families broach such things. Once, early on, I googled survival rates for those at her late stage of illness, and then snapped that window shut, incapable of accepting a truth so bald. My father became more ... patient, and the two of them have, in E's words, 'mellowed'.

While M prepared the dinner, I guided Mapa down the steep trail through scrubby bush to the rock pools, for a swim (I'd taken M the day before and shown him how the little rock-looking shells glued to the rock faces were actually alive and animal, and he had wanted to record it all on his iPhone, which annoyed me, but I tried not to let it show). At the foot of the trail, walkers and surfers had deposited their thongs, and this reminded me of people entering a house, or a mosque. Seaweed was bunched in great piles all along the shoreline, the bits that had been sitting in the sun turned black, which made them look like ash, or like the black leaves that had blown across to Marrickville from the fires in the mountains that summer.

Papa, predictably, stayed on the sand, reading his book, and I scoured the shore for the best shells, while Mama entered the water. She has always loved the water. Ever since I can remember I liked that moment when she would eventually re-emerge from the ocean, because she always looked different. Not just that her hair was nearly black or that her face was ruddied, but like she had been, however momentarily, unburdened. She looked for a flat spot of rock, to be able to put her special compression stocking back on, and she asked me, as she was getting dressed, if she'd shown me her scars from the surgery, and I said no, she hadn't, and she showed me the scar running across her thigh, and travelling all the way up to her crotch. It was delicate and white, no more pronounced or brutal-looking than those that line my sister's wrists.

There were dark hairs visible, in that crease (that I think is what other women call a bikini line?) and I was struck by how unselfconscious she was about her body, this intimate part of her body, exposing it to me with as little shame as kids show fresh scabs to one another.

And as I walked along the ocean back towards the house with them, I fell a little behind, and I was struck suddenly by their smallness. I always thought of my father as built of muscles, but now I saw that his frame was really only about the same size as my own, and my mother was a whole head shorter than him, and she had lost weight. She looked almost frail now, her legs strong still but her arms like they had lost all their muscle, and I wondered if I now weighed more than she did; if I took up a larger space.

How crazy, I thought, that these two small bodies could occupy so very much of my inner world.

If I am forced to think up analogies for this thing I do then I also think back to the enormous lawn we had as kids – large enough for our Kombi van to do a full circle around. Me and my sister lying on it for hours at a time, foraging for four-leaf clovers. The small thrill when we thought we'd spotted one, only to realise that it was actually just a regular three-leaf one with one of its neighbour's leaves overlapping. How we'd treasure the four-leaved ones, run screaming inside to present to our mother, and then guard them. If we found more than one in a particular patch, we'd get extra focused on that area, because – and I don't know how logical this is – you had the sense that there ought to be others like it nearby.

And what, you must be wondering, are the four-leaved equivalents on my head? Well, it is the *roots* of the hair that have fascinated and arrested me from the start. Not every hair I extract will have one attached – at most probably only one in ten – but I'm compelled to keep on pulling until I get one that does. There is no sure way of telling whether a hair has a root attached until it has been removed – though it is not pure 'luck' either, my fingers are able to intuit whereabouts on my head and which particular hairs are most likely to reward.

The roots themselves are pearl-white and translucent, cleave to the hair like muscle to a bone, and the very tips are black as can be. Belonging as they do to the subcutaneous world, but now brought into dry air, I cannot help but think of them as amphibious. Some roots are quite delicate, as though the tip of the hair has been dipped in and out of melted wax; others more swollen, like the eye of a needle; and others are fatter, almost maggoty-looking. If the hair is sturdy enough, then the small bead of root will sit atop, like an alfalfa sprout. But if the hair is more delicate, then it will loll with the root's weight, like a fishing rod does with its catch.

I find being under direct sunlight best of all, since the heat seems to soften the roots, making them slide out smoothly, almost viscous. I ought to add: the light itself is important, since each individual prize I must stare at, soberly as one might a fire's movements. Once I've gone to bed and obviously the light is off, then what I do is hold up each hair above me, against the window. There's an enormous monolith of an apartment block that hogs most of the view from my room; the side that faces me is a single flat featureless wall and it is against this blank plane that I hold up each hair, silhouetted, and that way I can ascertain whether or not the root is still attached. So when I walk or ride by the apartment block – 'Lume', it's called – I feel I know it intimately. Sometimes, when it's overcast or when occasionally I'm out camping (no windowpanes, no streetlight glow) then what I do each time I get one (because instinctively I *know*, when I have one) is press the side of my phone so that the screen lights up, hold the hair against it, determine its size and its precise shape.

And in this way, everything around me – windows, mobile phones, the sun and the moon – all get bound up in my strange compulsions, invested with secret purposes.

I remember, as kids, picking blades of grass. There was this one kind of grass where the different sections were folded around one another, so that several, thinner sections enveloped an internal, thicker section. To get to the middle bit, you couldn't just yank it out, you had to tug at it with just the right touch, and then it would slide out, revealing the root, whiter and slightly thicker. And the impulse was to take just the root between your teeth. It had a nice texture to it, and an oniony taste. What exactly was the appeal? Perhaps something instinctive; some primal satisfaction in having gathered something yourself, from the ground. 'Don't put that in your mouth! A dog could've pissed there!' adults would warn us. But didn't adults realise? The bits we put in our mouths were the hidden bits; the protected bits, that if not for our little fingers, would never have seen the light.

And with my hair, the instinct is to let the root rest against my bottom lip. You would think that something so subterranean ought to be warm to the touch, but believe me when I tell you that the roots are cold. Cold like metal, or like the lead of a pencil. And slightly slimy, but only for so long (a window of five minutes or so) and then they dry out.

The next instinct is to place the root between my teeth, close them just enough so as to be able to strip the root from the sheath, but not so tight as to actually break the hair. The taste is subtle: I've never needed to find a word to describe it but now that I do – not quite as salty as tears, and not metallic like blood, but brackish. Yes, brackish is the word. And then there are the even rarer crisp ones (where there's an ever-so-small dot of blood) – their texture is much the same as that of a kiwi-fruit seed, if you manage to pierce it right between your teeth.

The roots are what bring me the deepest pleasure and fullest absorption. But only from *inside* the experience, when the world is reduced to teeth and touch, and taste. When I take a step back, and imagine looking in from the *outside*, I think: what I'm doing must look masochistic, deviant, repulsive. And that imagining brings me immense shame.

Recently, by which I mean for at least the past year, every so often a hair I've pulled is white. These hairs, thick and white as dental floss, shocked me twofold – the first was the same shock that I imagine must register with anyone when they notice white hair in the mirror the first time. But for me the real shock was this: that I have been pulling so long my hair has had time to turn white. Still, I tried to deny this reality by convincing myself that these were just an anomaly – some kind of albino growth, that didn't signify anything. But I couldn't deny the fact that these white strays appeared between my fingers with more and more frequency. Still they weren't so many – perhaps one in two hundred at most. I came to use them as a signal, to incorporate them into my own weird internal system. Like some kind of wildcard in a deck of cards, I decided that when one appeared, *that* was the moment I must stop.

Though of course it doesn't work like that, the resolution to stop. I've been unable to stop for so long now that in the same way a guitarist's fingertips eventually grow worn or grooved in places from the pressure of the strings, my right index finger has developed a squareness to it, as though it were made of plasticine, not flesh.

I can feel, here, my impulse to explain something to you; to tell you that these compulsions are not my own crazy invention. For some reason I think people are readier to believe and to sympathise when they are told something has a name. And part of me wants your sympathy, of course it does, but there would be something false about it, too. For in the two years either side of my eighteenth birthday, when my compulsions were taking hold in me, I had no name for what I was doing; it never even occurred to me that what I was doing was a *thing*.

And so I want to honour that girl's not-knowing, though maybe not-knowing is the wrong way of thinking about it. At the time I felt like the knowing one. I had always been secretive and separate, but now these facets of me intensified, so that without anyone else's being aware of it, my life became two-pronged. I continued to live my visible life, the one in which I studied hard and baked cakes and visited the library. But parallel to this, my second, secret, silent life took hold.

# INSIDE AN EPISODE

In the same way that my loose hairs knit themselves into my woollen jumpers, the memory of my pulling attaches itself to the places I inhabit. The places that ought to feel the safest of all and the homeliest and the most intimate – my house, my bed – become steeped in my memory of what I have done there. Even when – rarely – these places are clean to the eye, they feel saturated with my own haunting shame.

My shame by now feels self-evident. But if I had to articulate it, I'd say its real locus is that all this is – ostensibly – my own doing. *I* am the one who tears the hair from my head and then savours each slick root. *I* remove it from where it belongs and feed it to where it does not, so that the roots which belong in my scalp end up on my lips, in my mouth, in my stomach. I mean, who *does* that? If my hair had fallen out 'naturally', or if it had been a side-effect from some sort of medical treatment, I don't believe I would feel half the amount of shame I do.

I'm ashamed too of how my compulsions have got so out of hand and have expanded to be such a large a part of 'me'. I'm ashamed that I am unable to stop. And, maybe most painfully of all, I'm ashamed of my own shame. We're encouraged, now, to feel pride towards those aspects of our identities that might in times past have been deemed shameful (our fatness, our sexuality, our kinks) but I am so stuck with my shame. It feels socially unacceptable; taboo; as though it belongs to an earlier, mediaeval time.

At times in my life, this has become so unbearable that I've needed to physically escape. I spent the four years of my degree in four separate locations: my family home in Richmond; a rambling share-house in Enmore; an international student residence in La Rochelle; a second share-house in Glebe; and each time I moved, it was such a physical relief to start afresh, to have a clean space, and to believe that I might be able to *be* clean in all senses of the word.

When I left Sydney in 2010 to volunteer teaching English to asylum seekers on Christmas Island, I explained it to people by saying I thought I'd find the work rewarding; and then when I accepted the subsequent offer to work in remote Western Australia, I told people this work felt nothing short of a calling. None of this was untrue, but there were other reasons, underneath these, that I didn't reveal to anyone. I was desperate to be better. I thought that if I put as much distance as possible between me and the places that I had pulled, I could shuck the sickness off myself; relinquish it, finally, for good.

I considered detainees' struggles and sadnesses real and

warranted. Naively, I thought that if I spent long enough in their presence, bearing witness to their plight, then I would be jolted out of my my own self-constructed sadness and my self-inflicted harm.

But inevitably, my habits would pursue me. In the pet-less terrace house I moved into in 2013, I remember a flatmate singing out while mopping the bathroom floor: 'Guys? One of us is *molting*.'

Like anyone who owns an animal can tell you, hair gets everywhere. Wherever I was, I was incapable of keeping a single surface unsullied by pieces of myself. I have wondered whether there is some underlying impulse: to mark my territory in the same way a dog does his? To make it mine? To make it home?

Now, I've grown used to knowing where I'm up to in a discarded book by the fur-length curls collected together in the crease of a page. When I return to my laptop I've grown used to blowing with as much force as a kid at a (pre-Covid) birthday cake at the haze that sits three-dimensional over the lower half of the keyboard. Like Hansel and Gretel's breadcrumbs, my hairs trail me, small signs of my movements and of my state of mind, evidence of each place abandoned or escaped.

For a long time, I thought that my habits were like desire lines – those unofficial paths that establish themselves in bushland, by virtue of the passing of animals: the more used they are, the more established they become. In a way, I was right: the paths we trace in our thinking strengthen the connections between neurons, so that they become – quite literally – grooved into our brains. But my mistake was in thinking that if I were to displace my body into a new setting, then I might be able to forge new paths. Now, I know this to be a fantasy. Now, I know that my deeply grooved brain is with me, wherever I am. It is a place unto itself. Like a child's secret spot, the power of this place lies less in its specific features or contours, and more in the fact of its location being hidden, the fact that no-one else knows where it is, or how to get there, or is able to access it. In short: it is the place where only I can go.

I *always* start off in full control (this may be an illusion, but who can say?). The set sequence of probing-stroking-pulling-examining cannot be interrupted, and is totally absorbing, but between the end of that chain and the beginning of the next (that is, locating the next hair) there is a definite gap. This gap could be enough time to read a whole paragraph, could be enough time to make a cup of tea, can sometimes even be enough time for me to stop pulling altogether. But then incrementally, these gaps shorten, or in other words, each fluid sequence comes closer and closer on the heels of the one before it until the gaps are so infinitesimal that everything blurs into one unbroken loop.

You know when you're entering the ocean, there comes a definite point where you go from being able to touch the bottom with your feet to not being able to, where you're *just* out of your depth? It's like that, and once I'm at that threshold things escalate. Instead of selecting individual hairs, often what happens is I'll begin to pull two at a time, then three or four, and then small tufts. What I do, too, is take note of the ratio of rootless hairs to ones with roots attached. So if, say, there's approximately one root in seven then I pull seven hairs out at a time so as to maximise the chances of one root per pull. (This all sounds very deliberate and mathematical, I know, but I ought to add that this all happens unthinkingly. It may also sound painful, but it honestly is not.)

Sometimes when I pull out a small bunch together the hairs will stand parallel, like tightly bunched long stem roses, and other times they'll come out splayed. And then I will – subconsciously again – shift what it is I am looking for. A root will no longer be satisfying. I'll decide – or perhaps *know* is a better choice of word here – that I now need a root of a particular size, a certain fatness. Sometimes recently I've discovered a patch of relatively dense growth on the back part of my scalp; the density gives me permission to pull – just a split second of permission, mind you, but that's all I require – and I pull a tuft and maybe six or seven of the ten have roots attached, some stuck to one another so they look almost gelatinous. And then I can feel my whole being stop, the same hushing-heart-stopping feeling I have felt on entering a high-ceilinged church.

In this way I have been held captive for hours at a time. I have seventeen *years'* worth of exercise books dedicated especially to trying to discern the shape of this thing, in all its vagaries, and if I were to open one of these diaries now to any random day I could tell you precisely what time I started pulling and for how many minutes and in what circumstances, and my physical location, and my mood preceding. But I find it too painful returning to those pages; the indignity of it.

Suffice to say: there have been days when I have spent more hours in this state than not. Thinking about that fills me with grief.

So captive is this state that from within it I have watched my phone ring on the carpet beside me, but been incapable of reaching across to pick it up. In my laundry, which adjoins the lounge room, once I accidentally forgot to unplug the sink that the machine drains into, and listened to the sink fill then flood, knowing – at some level – that it must be seeping into the carpet, but helpless to interrupt it. When I've been overtaken, I have stood and watched water in my porridge simmer away into the air, and then the oats turn black and crackle with dryness, and my ears fill with the smoke alarm's shriek.

In one particular incarnation that has stuck in my mind: in 2018 I was at a writers' residency in Virginia of all places, believing that if I put as much distance as possible between myself and my home, I'd be able to write about my afflictions with more perspective, and also be better able to banish the censorious eyes that were always hovering over me when I wrote, that filled me with shame. And, no doubt, inwardly I hoped I could break the habit once and for all.

I'd avoided the residency's lake for the first week or so, since some of the other residents had heard you could get E. coli, but one other resident like me didn't seem deterred and the water was just too inviting. So we had a little system going where once it got to a point in the afternoon that she was up for a swim she'd just knock on my door. I know this doesn't sound very amazing but in this age of social media, and where the only people who knocked at doors were electricity providers or Jehovah's witnesses, it felt somehow precious. The lake was way better than the gym that, with its sterile squash courts and its empty running track, had something tragic about it, like those photos of abandoned malls ... An old boat shed sat on the edge of the lake, wooden and rotting and dilapidated in a way the rest of the campus wasn't.

I'm the type who usually takes a good twenty minutes to reach the deeper water, and needs to let each part of my body adjust to the temperature before I inch in any further. But here the piers jutted out so you couldn't enter the water from the bay, and so I had no choice but to enter all at once.

Back in my room in the two hours we had before dinner (meals were at a set time) – more than enough time to shower and change and 'chill' – I found myself pulling compulsively. I was kneeling on the carpet as I did so, sitting back on my haunches (is that what they're called?) as though supplicating, feet tucked under my bum. Within minutes one foot got pins and needles but still I kept on. And eventually instead of removing my foot from under me (by this stage it was entirely numb) what I did to take the pressure off that foot was to tip myself backwards, so that I was on my back with my legs tucked up beneath me; and still I kept on, bringing tufts of hair to my eye level, shoving the chosen ones into my mouth. The position brought to mind that of a cockroach that's just been sprayed; upturned and limbs flailing trying to get upright.

I heaved myself to dinner only slightly late, too dazed even to worry like I normally did about the fact that what I had done must be leaking out of me.

How to explain to the other residents that the reason I was still wet with lake-water was that in my bedroom I had become more insect than human?

How to explain in my emails to people back home that in this space on the other side of the world I had been given to nurture my mind, instead I was preoccupied with the contortions of my body?

For now, I have described enough of what was happening on the external surface of my scalp, and I want to tell you a little bit about what was happening beneath its surface. Of course it is never easy to disentangle the physical from the mental, and least of all in my own case, when the two are in such close proximity to one another. I find it so weird to think of my hair follicles embedded in the deepest layer of skin, and beneath that a layer of skull, and not far beneath that, right *there*: a brain, and somewhere within that, that thing we call *mind*.

As physical as my strange afflictions are, it is in the mind that the deepest mystery occurs.

How to characterise my usual state of mind? In the presence of other people I am intensely self-conscious. Alone, my thoughts tend to the ruminative and the obsessive. Frenetic; like when you've got too many computer tabs open at once; attention darting between one thing and the next, never settling. Thoughts, and then thoughts about those thoughts, ad infinitum. Is this jumbled state, overstimulated and yet always craving more stimulus, a peculiarly modern condition?

I am sure anyone who has attempted meditation or anyone in possession of a brain will recognise this kind of monkeyish mind.

I have grown used to conceiving of time as something that is in short supply, and that I must be careful not to squander. To tell the truth, I have come to fear empty pockets of time ... I am afraid to daydream, to let my thoughts wander, because there is always the same risk: that it leads me to pulling.

I need, at all costs, to stay alert. There are two particular thoughts that feel on a constant simmer: *Just pull one; don't dare start pulling*. It's not that I lurch between these magnetic urges and the fierce resistance to those urges; rather I hold the two simultaneously. The tension that results between the two occupies much of my mind (and I can feel it in my body, too, this stiffness, I am like the little bubble in one of those spirit levels that builders use to check how flat a surface is, sensitive to even the slightest of tilts that risk sending me careening).

At some inevitable point – a lapse in attention, a fatiguing – and I will be lured into pulling, just the one hair to begin. And then the set of thoughts I hold will be something like: *Just one more; don't dare pull any more; why did you start?; you shouldn't have started, now you won't be able to stop; just stop now*. To be clear, there is no voice from above, no competing voices vying for my attention ... it is *my* voice alone that I am hearing. Though actually, now I think about it, I don't know that *voice* is the right word for it either. There are no words involved. Perhaps all this is more akin to feeling than thought.

At some point, I go from feeling that messages are being sent back and forth between my brain and my fingers, to feeling that I have no choice but to surrender, not to my own physical urges this time, but to some other unseen force. After over a decade of visiting me, these forces have the power to awe me still.

I have come to think of this point of surrender as a *turning*.

Physically, it is true I am pulling out my hair.

Mentally, I slip from this world into another one.

It's not quite a slip from consciousness into unconsciousness, because I am conscious the entire time, I think, but the quality of the consciousness is distinct: softer, immersive, expansive. And each time I make this crossing, I feel I have *arrived*. Within the forest, a sudden glade.

And though I have reached this place and inhabited it thousands upon thousands of times, know my way there like I know the back of my literal hand, still this sensation of arrival never loses its intensity.

If I don't visit for some time, then when I do, it feels nothing less than a homecoming. And each time I'm relieved, that things are just as I left them; intact.

It's not true to say I cease to be aware of the pulling; I am cognisant of it, but it becomes semi-automatic – in the same way that legs in deep water will know to keep on treading.

Is the mind able to focus on more than one thing at a time? I have heard said that multitasking is a myth; that in actuality our attention can only rest on one thing at a time, though it can flit between two or more things. Maybe that is what happens? Flitting? Though it *feels* like I am holding two things at a time.

The analogy that comes to mind is of playing the piano – which don't they say uses both sides of the brain? When I had to learn a new piece, first I'd practise the two hands separately; typically the left is usually more straightforward (more predictable, a succession of chords to underpin and tether the melody) whereas the right is typically more fluid – florid, even – cascading and rippling. Once I had the left hand part more or less under control, then I would bring in the right hand over the top, tentative at first, but increasingly fluent, until the two parts came to sound as one.

So, you might think of the action of pulling as somehow equivalent to the pianist's left hand: minimal attention required, but still always operating, ceaseless, fundamental in underpinning everything. And then what is happening in some other part of my head while this pulling carries on relentless, might be thought of as a kind of right-handed 'melody'. Each part distinct, but parts of the same whole.

So once I get into a rhythm of pulling, it is not that my thoughts dissipate exactly, but what does happen is that I feel forced up against the stream of awareness itself. Rather than different thoughts all jostling for attention, I am able to discern one strand of thought, which reveals itself as cleanly as a fishbone lifted from its surrounding flesh. This strand of thought distinguishes itself not only in its purity but in its fluidity: roaming and cartwheeling and leaping like a creature released.

With piano, once a piece has been sufficiently practised so there are no stumbles, no hesitations, then your attention is able to hover somewhere that is neither quite directed to the right nor to the left hand, and yet manages to encompass the two.

As a child, I was never one for talking about my innermost feelings. But when I played the piano all that pent-up emotion that I didn't realise was pent-up seeped out into the music. I could get so transported by the music – invariably haunting pieces in minor keys – that often I felt it was betraying me; exposing me. Teachers and adjudicators would remark on the immense feeling I was able to convey, though it was my mother who would comment most often; I would practise as she prepared the dinner, and it seemed to appease something in her.

Arrived, I feel in communion with the self in a way I never otherwise do; my usual self-consciousness doesn't just fade but evaporates without trace. Time itself dissolves. Truth be told *I* seem to evaporate, and in my wake, something unnameable I have broken through to. A kind of *grace*.

And here is the deepest paradox of all: that only here – in complete submission to my urges – do I feel truly freed of them.

This might all sound like an escape from what we like to call 'reality', which I suppose in some way it is, but to me it has never felt that way. It has always felt like an encounter; I have the sense of a faculty regained; like this is how my mind is *meant* to work.

If someone were to witness my movements and gestures

surely the word they would use is 'repetitive' and yet when I am *there*, it doesn't feel monotonous or mechanical. No two visits are ever the same. Like a surfer can keep on returning to the same stretch of coastline, I keep on coming back, because it's never quite the same place.

I ought to add that these images of pianos and surfers are ones that I am coming up with after the fact, and I know they are unsatisfying ones. I have never until now been tempted to draw any analogy; my pulling just *is*.

Does detailing all this for you make any difference to my experience; has it slowed it down at all? Well, in truth it has done little to weaken my compulsions. But let me tell you here about a girl – a woman I suppose, British, a little older than me, but the two of us shared what she called an 'ingenue' look. I met her at Varuna, the writers' house in the Blue Mountains, and since she'd never set foot in this hemisphere, I offered to take her for a walk into the bush. She was the kind of person who'd read copious amounts about our flora and fauna and history and geography before arriving here. Her delight of recognition was plain: all these things she'd seen in print now made physical: 'Oh, that must be *grevillea*!' 'And is that *banksia*, the one named after Joseph Banks?' 'Do you think we might see any *cockatoos*? Or a *lyrebird*?'

Since mapping out the mechanics of my pulling on paper, sometimes I, too, experience those same little bursts of recognition. Oh, now my fingers are *prowling*; and oh here comes the *turning*. And, oh now I have *arrived*. As circular and as absurd as that may sound to you, still these moments of recognition are consolation to me: at least I have succeeded in pinning down some slivers of my experience onto the page. Even if all these words do precious little to soften my compulsions, still that consolation is important to me.

But ultimately, my experience of being transported into spacelessness and timelessness is not something I feel equipped to communicate adequately. I have tried to sketch its edges for you, but its heart remains something unknowable; a thing sublime.

I wish that I could describe one of my rhapsodic thoughts to you in some detail ...

From within the midst of an episode, I will often vow to capture my thinking on paper as *soon* as my hands are capable of holding a pen. But it seems to be one of the features of this thought that it always manages to resist being pinned down. Trying to remember details afterwards is like trying to recall a dream you had several months ago.

I am ensnared, I need to let the impulse run its course (while breaking through the partition in one direction is all too easy, the reverse is near-insurmountable) and as it does so, my state of mind slides from feeling epiphanic into a syrupy state of exhaustion. My physical state slows, too; like a marathon runner I am still making the same movements but in slower motion, drawing on some different, deeper reserve of strength.

If on arrival I feel I've regained some faculty, now it seems all my systems have shut down bar whatever faculty it is that's responsible for my fingers pulling hair after hair after hair, as though my body had mistaken it for the pumping of my heart; a thing that must never cease. I have in fact been trapped in this state in my own bed, in the hours when I ought to have been sleeping.

What happens now is the thoughts come in flickers: *Is that the sound of a mosquito? / it's getting dark already / my back hurts / I'm cold.* In other words, they are thoughts as base as an animal's. There are slits of opportunity wherein I can decide to heave myself out, finally, but these moments are all too easy to miss.

I feel, at the end of an episode, that I've been shipwrecked: dazed and conspicuously fragile.

If I've been pulling on the train home then it's such a struggle to get from the train station home, a flat, three-and-a-half minute walk. I'll call M to come and collect me (I have had to do this a humiliating number of times, in the six years we have lived here). If he isn't home, though, then sometimes I lean my elbow against the button at the lights (just to support my body), and once I cross the road, rest on the low-lying brick wall, walking as though swimming fully-clothed.

When I pull too long, stay in that state too long, my teeth start to chatter like a child stayed in cold water too long. Sometimes when M gets home, he finds me like that, teeth chattering no matter if it's the middle of summer, no matter how uncold my body is, and part of me is grateful for the sound of teeth on teeth. I cannot speak in this state — if I try my words are slurred and anyway the sound of bone on bone communicates better than I could. Nobody has ever seen me in this state except for him (and even if they did, they could not guess at how I had reached it). When I reach this point I am too exhausted, incapable even of shame. I am reverted to some primitive, infant need, to be soothed and held tight.

Having lost all sense of time, I have emerged from an episode incapable of telling whether I have been gone for twenty minutes or two hours. It is like the sensation of waking from a jet-lagged sleep, those split seconds of needing to consciously situate yourself back in time and space. And as with any extended flight, it can take a little while to feel you have actually arrived.

Often I don't know exactly what time I commenced, and so I have devised little methods to work out how much time has passed ... There is always the sky; occasionally, after a severe episode I will see with a shock: dark has fallen. But with less severe episodes I have found pressing my finger against the side of my mug of tea useful: many episodes I have found last as long as it takes tea to turn cold. The other useful measure is if I have something in the oven, and I remove it, which makes me feel a bit like one of those chefs on TV who, thanks to the time lapse, transform something raw into something golden in the space of seconds. Though sometimes when I remove my creation it is verging on burnt.

I am struggling to translate all this to you; when I am not in the midst of it I myself struggle to fathom it. Such is the strangeness of all this that – once I have returned to the world – I find it difficult to contemplate or believe in its subsuming power. It seems outlandish, which I suppose in the strictest sense of the word, it is, since like I have said, it is as though I enter a land unto itself. Like when I've been about to fly into a European winter, and have stood in an op-shop in the Australian summer trying on woollen jumpers and scarves, try as I might, I can't really imagine so many layers being half-necessary. But when I am in the throes of it, seized by it, then it is all there is. It can swallow days whole, swallow me whole.

Weirdly enough, sometimes I am grateful for the physical evidence of my condition, because otherwise I know that I myself would find it hard to believe where it was I'd been. Even though I go to extraordinary lengths to keep my pulling secret, still I trust that if, hypothetically, I were to show someone (*anyone*) my un-bobby-pinned head they would see in an instant that something was clearly awry. It is all solid proof. I pity those whose sufferings are wholly invisible. I'm glad at least I have proof, that at least I can't second-guess *myself* about this.

So bewitching is the act of pulling; so entrancing the place it takes me to ... and yet, the *not*-pulling consumes as much of my mind as the pulling does. The constant transitioning between states of pulling and not-pulling is what shapes and textures my days ... I don't know what a day would even look like without these vagaries. On any given day, before pulling, comes the latent state, forward-looking: I am determined not to pull. I am vigilant; this vigilance has become embedded in me, so that in conversation I am defensive, guarded, on edge, untrusting of outward calm, because I know how swiftly things can turn. And having pulled, I am vigilant still, since it is all the more difficult to resist pulling once I have already started – my defences feel depleted. On the rare days – or, even rarer, strings of days – where I manage not to pull at all, then I feel a secret surge of strength. But even on these days, I still like to gather a tuft – when the tuft is a certain size then there is no real risk of anything coming out – just to feel the pull of it against my scalp. And I feel glad to have something to hold onto; to tether me.

I am hyper-conscious of which stage of this cycle I am in; I can't help but measure my days according to how successful my resistance has been.

Even when I haven't dwelt there for some time, still it feels right *there*. The place where words count for nothing, where will counts for nothing: I am always on the brink of that chasm. I imagine many people are able to go about their lives on dry land; I feel as though I am always paddling in that space where *here* I can touch the ground, but just *there* I can't. Or does everyone have these kind of surreal, unrecorded, and unrepeatable pockets to their lives? Does everyone go places and come back and hide where exactly it is they've been? Sometimes I convince myself they must, so that I might feel less alone.

# OTHER PEOPLE

In my first year of university, my pulling got to the stage where if my hair was wet the damage I'd done was very obvious. So, I figured, I had to avoid others seeing me with wet hair at all costs. I'd go weeks without washing my hair, and if my mother berated me I'd have to pretend I'd washed it while she was out, or wash it and then make an excuse to stay in my bedroom until it dried. At the local pool, on scorching hot days, I'd have to invent reasons not to go in the water, or claim not to feel the heat.

I'd try to avoid anyone ever seeing me in direct sunlight, or too close to a light. When the damage was at its worst – when almost my entire scalp was insubstantial as a dandelion head, and what hair remained me had to be arranged into a fastidious comb-over – I'd try not to ever let anyone ever see from behind. I was worried their eyes might rest on the back of my head and so I would make sure to angle my body in such a way as to avoid turning my back to them when I walked away by doing a weird sideways kind of scuttling walk, like a crab. I didn't like eye contact at the best of times, but I was also hypervigilant about anyone's gaze drifting anywhere above my eyes, towards my forehead, or my hairline – if I sensed it was then I would spring up out of the blue, to increase the distance between their eyes and my hair, and feign fetching something from somewhere.

I've always had a fierce need for secrecy. It's always felt like second nature to me, this guarding of things that perhaps needn't have been guarded.

Before I got my period Mama had taken me aside to give me some pads in preparation. At the time, there were none of the nice leopard print or paisley packaging – this was plain, sterile. She opened one out and told me she'd got the ones with 'wings' and I acted like I knew what she meant, squirming to escape the conversation but acting nonchalant, as though she'd bought me a new set of exercise books. Later, alone, I remember unfolding one, positioning it at different angles like a tangram, baffled by the sticky bits – should they stick to your skin?

I was twelve when I had my menarche. I remember that day still: it was raining, and there were snail tracks everywhere on the concrete floor of the backyard toilet, and Mama said, gently: 'It's raining in your body, too.' I didn't *decide* to hide future periods, it wasn't a deliberate thing; it just seemed easier; natural. I'd read in some smuggled edition of *Dolly* (smuggled because I'd have considered it embarrassing to display any curiosity in typical 'girly' things) that it could be good to signal to those around you when you were at 'that time of the month', by, say, tying a red handkerchief to your bedpost. Just the *idea* of this made me wince. I think at some level I resented the idea Mama would judge or assess me using this knowledge, so that if I got upset at her (for yet another of her endless tirades) she'd turn it back on me, put it down to my having my period.

But separate from that, my blood – and my understanding of its patterns – belonged to *me* and this struck me as important. So when I had my period I'd pretend I didn't, and other times pretend I had it when I didn't ... for a period of several *years* I stuffed stained knickers into my wardrobe, until it got to the point where at age sixteen – my cycle being so erratic – my mother made an appointment for me to see a specialist. And then, magically, my period returned of its own accord, with perfect regularity.

My sister and I were not the kind of 'pasty' kids to get sick much, a fact my mother repeated often. We talked about kids with allergies and eczema as though theirs was a moral failing. My mother would tell us how she kept on working – climbing the ladder with kilos of fruit strapped to her chest – right up until E's birth. With similar pride, she'd remind us that when Papa was doing his military service, so fit and tireless was he that he'd be given extra guns to carry.

We told ourselves our family was robust and this was, perhaps, a necessary narrative. In the jobs my parents worked, there was no such thing as sick leave: a day spent resting was a day of money lost, and it has taken me many years to unlearn this way of thinking. (My mother works in an office now, and she's incredulous at the amount of sick leave written into her contract; incredulous, too, at those who use it too frequently for her liking.)

I didn't visit the dentist for the entirety of my twenties, another fact I hid from my mother, who would check every few months how recently I'd been. The longer I left it, the more afraid I was – afraid not only of the prospect of physical pain, but how any dentist would judge me; what the state of my teeth might expose about the state of my mind. I didn't know how to explain that sometimes, the effort of brushing my teeth was beyond me. Or that sometimes I entered the bathroom to do my teeth, and an hour later, sink strewn with hair and toothbrush still dry, I gave up and had to go to bed teeth unbrushed?

I've always hidden my thoughts, and tried my best to conceal my feelings. In primary school, while the other kids would clamour to have their turn at show and tell, I refused to ever participate (and I wonder now, why no teacher ever found this troubling). 'For Chrissake, I have to squeeze any conversation out of you,' my mother would complain. Words come through my hand far more fluently than through my mouth, though even writing appeals to me the most when I do it furtively. Some stages in my life I reckon I've probably written more words than I've spoken, which is not to say that I've written all that much, just that my silence can be extreme, and unsettling to people. My silence is part of the collection of things that line me with shame. Occasionally someone will describe me as 'private' or 'elusive' and even this throws me, that someone should so much as suspect me of having secrets.

Despite the lengths I took to guard my most secret of secrets, in that first year of uni the damage I'd done was beyond being able to be concealed. Those around me began to notice. Sitting beside my sister on car-trips, I'd forbid myself from dozing off at all, because who knew how my hairstyle might get ruffled in my sleep. Once, though, I couldn't stay awake the whole trip, and my scrupulous arrangement must have started to come undone. I remember E pointing out a bald section of my scalp and laughing, and me using all my big-sister authority to make her shush. Another time that year, I remember being outside with Papa, pruning young roses in the nursery where he worked, and I think I must have been at that stage where I was still in a kind of denial about just how obvious was the damage I'd done and he must, I'm sure, have been under the influence of Mama's prodding to *try to talk* to me. 'Your hair's all *patchy*, like mine,' he said. I shouldn't wear it tied up so tight all the time, he said; I should wear it out: he said hair needs to breathe, and that I should let it get more sunlight.

One evening that same year I remember Mama coming into my bedroom, when I was lying on my bed. (I have memories as far back as I can remember, of crying inconsolably, of her comforting me, but the cause of my tears being a mystery to the both of us.) My tears have always felt burdensome to me, and I was afraid to burden my mother with anything. The boundary between us was brittle; I knew that even the hint of my pain would hurt her, and so it felt less like I was keeping secrets safe from her, and more that it was *her* I was protecting. Neither of us knew how to handle tears, other than to make them stop, as though they were a leaking tap that needed tamping, and I hated the distance that this widened up between us. She sat on the edge of the bed, reached out and started stroking my hair, so gentle that I was ashamed of my own impulse to cower. 'You're losing hair.' She made me promise to talk to the doctor about it. 'It could be something *permanent*.' Now, I see these moments as turning points missed, and wonder what could have been, if I had let anyone help. At the time, though, they only prompted one thought: *I need to cover my tracks better*.

One of the most mysterious aspects of this entire phenomenon is how those around me, as though my own shame were contagious, colluded in my secret. That first year of uni I began to dread meeting relatives I hadn't seen in some time, because change that happens incrementally can go unnoticed, but to those who saw me only months apart, the change in my appearance was far more obvious. I distinctly recall a relative asking my mother directly in front of me: 'What's Adele *done* to her *hair*?' and my mother covering for me: 'That's just how she likes to wear it, bunched up.'

When it comes to the question of why neither of my parents made more of a concerted attempt to address my hair-pulling or my depressive state ... My first instinct is to leap to their defence and to explain away: I was living out of home by the time my compulsions were most severe, and pretty well anything can be hidden from someone you only see in person for a handful of hours at a time; I am a private person, and practised at concealing much of myself – so how were they to guess?

And even once it got to the point where the damage could no longer be successfully hidden, how could they have known *how* the damage had came about? And so, even in those moments of exposure in which I burned with shame, my *real* secret always felt safe.

But I suppose it *is* curious, how unskilled my parents seem to be at reading me, and how very much of myself I am so adept at hiding from them. And when I think a bit harder about it, I see that this has always been so. Countless times when I'd come home from school in high spirits Mama would ask why I was so irritable; other times I'd have been crying and this didn't appear to register with her. She'll ask if I'm okay at random moments; she doesn't seem to clock when something she's said has hurt or offended me; she often misses my sarcasm; she chides us for joking about things that in her opinion we shouldn't.

To her credit: once, when she was alone with M, she told him that I was losing hair. I think she said it like she'd taken it upon herself to notify him of something he mightn't be aware of? (In actual fact, and as you'll come to see, he not only understood the particularities of my illness like nobody else, but had become entwined with and implicated in it.) Afterwards, he told me what she'd said, adding: 'She really does care about you, you can see it in her eyes.' But it had never occurred to me that she didn't care – only that she cared excessively.

Because here's the thing: underneath everything, my

mother is deeply sensitive. A lawnmower in the distance, or the rustle of a plastic bag, or a faint smell that no-one else can detect will leave her agitated. Like me, she is incapable of watching violence in movies; she has a natural sympathy for the downtrodden; if we are at a picnic table somewhere, she will fret that the other families arriving mightn't have enough shade.

At the beach, when we were kids and while our cousins surfed, E and I would sit building sandcastles of intricate design, wetting the sand just enough that it could be dripped by hand into small towers, and she would admire our work with great seriousness. I remember she'd get upset – not outwardly, but personally – at other children, boys, typically, who'd jump on the sandcastles their female counterparts had built, or who threw sand, or who were chasing after the pigeons or seagulls with sticks.

Two years ago, M and I hosted Christmas in our tiny apartment, and on Boxing Day I rode over to my sister's, where my parents had stayed the night. Papa, in his sometimes awkward way of starting conversations, asked me if we'd got through all the many dishes from the night before.

'Yeah, *and* we vacuumed, 'cause M took those bottles out of the laundry sink and sat them on top of the washing machine to dry, and then he put a load on. Anyway we went up the road for a coffee and when we came back there was glass everywhere. Even in the lounge room. And all the carpet was soggy with those bloody Vodka Cruisers.'

I tell this story expecting it to be amusing (they knew I'd found an entire unopened box of Vodka Cruisers in a skip a few days before, and I'd lugged them home) but instead Mama's face turns grave and ashen.

'Oh, *Adele*.'

'It's not the end of the world, Mama, it's only Vodka Cruisers! And it's not like I paid for them.'

'But still.' And she tuts, her face showing the news still sinking in. The carelessness; the waste; the imagined mess of it all.

I think to myself: *Oh, if only she knew*.

A weird kind of collusion operated around my sister also. At the time my compulsions were taking serious hold, she was in her early teens. Up the insides of her arms, there began to appear what looked like giant cigarette burns. If asked about it, she'd say matter-of-factly she'd burnt herself ironing, even though we were not the kind of family to iron our clothes much. I remember feeling ... what was it? A perverse kind of satisfaction, I think: that she had plainly done something *wrong*, the same shade of shock as when she once told Papa to his face to 'piss off', that she had transgressed. Ours was not a religious family but it felt to me like something sacrilegious. I think I felt a kind of anger at what I saw then as her ingratitude: couldn't she see our parents were already struggling enough without adding this to their plates?

It must have come up between me and Mama (not, if I'm honest, out of genuine concern, but more a desire to get her into trouble) but Mama repeating to me the same explanation about the iron. I don't know how convinced of this she was;

was she protecting me, or protecting E's privacy, or did she *need* to believe E's unlikely words because the alternative was too painful for her to contemplate? I don't know what precipitated it, but at some point E got taken to see the school counsellor, who reported back to Mama, who reported back to me the counsellor's conclusion: she was one 'very sad girl'. My mother related this information in the way that we'd sometimes read aloud lines of one another's horoscopes in the Saturday paper. It was cryptic information from someone who didn't know what they were on about. I don't know what conversations my mother and sister had around all this (and as for my father, I suspect he'd have been saddened by the knowledge of his daughter's sadness, but also find it unfathomable). Along with confusion, I wonder if my mother also felt a degree of shame; that she herself hadn't realised the depth of E's sadness; that she had in some important way fallen short in her role as mother.

My sister was insanely beautiful at that age, and she put great effort into her presentation: velvets, eyeliner, elaborate jewellery. Often people would be taken aback when I introduced her as my sister. Other times people would ask if we were related, and comment on how alike we looked, which always made me so flattered, but I could tell made her cringe. I think people – adults above all – were blinded by her appearance, couldn't see past it (in the same way I think my academic excellence was the ultimate disguise). I used to get annoyed when she'd visit that first share-house I moved into, so ethereal and vacant-looking she'd become, and afterwards one housemate or another would comment on her appearance: 'Stunning.' I remember a friend's mother, a painter, saying how she would love to just sit down and paint her. 'I mean, you're pretty, too, but your *sister*, she ... she presents herself like a picture.'

I'm afraid there isn't much more I can fill in about my sister and her sorrow, partly because I have never asked her about that time, and partly because it is her story to tell. She is what I've heard people describe as 'chill', but every so often she admits to me that this is largely a facade. The other day she mentioned having just watched that Amy Winehouse documentary, and as she said it her eyes grew teary, and I tried my best to look as though I hadn't noticed (what is it, this familial impulse of ours, to hide any glimmer of vulnerability?) She has an enormous vegetable garden (my father when he sees her pottering says it reminds him so much of his own mother), and makes ceramics, and has a part-dingo dog that she says is the best thing she's ever done for what she calls her 'mental health' (when she said that I tried not to show my offence, that a dog could do more good than any of us humans). Yindi is by turns playful and placid; the only sound she reacts to is the shriek of black cockatoos, so prehistoric, my sister says, that it seems to awaken something ancient in her blood.

A few months back she picks me up in her battered RAV4, its dashboard cluttered with driftwood, and feathers, and snakeskins she found on a trip to Oberon, where each autumn she goes foraging for mushrooms. We head to Callan Park, a place whose beauty we both appreciate as one of the few pockets of the inner city not yet gentrified or 'developed': enormous rambling grounds with jacarandas and ancient-looking Moreton Bay figs; crumbling sandstone buildings, asbestos signs plastered over their windows. At one spot in the bay Yindi goes for a swim, and we spot some slimy eel-ish body not very far out, which panics E on Yindi's behalf.

Yindi must cover about ten times as much ground as we do, tearing around like a kid on a new scooter. She's supposed to stop before crossing roads but E each time has to call her back and remind her that she's meant to 'sit', which she does, but it's a bit tokenistic, and then she sprints off again. E says on account of her dingo-ness she can't be *too* firm with her – that might make other dogs more obedient but not Yindi, it's just the opposite. We wonder out loud what goes through Yindi's mind: how, for example, does she imagine the car works? Does she realise E is its driver?

E seems very adult; content; and it is good to see her in her element. But I can't know which secrets she keeps from me. (More than once on the drive home from visiting our parents, she has begun crying mid-conversation, and I see that despite sharing more of herself with our parents than I ever could, somewhere in her lies the impulse I know well: to protect them. I am glad that she feels safe to cry in my presence, at least.)

When she gives the nod to another dog-walker I tell her she's become a 'dog person'.

'I can't *stand* dog people,' she says.

I know that many siblings grow apart with age, but in our case it feels we are only now coming to know one another properly, only now beginning to bridge the terrible distance that marked our relationship as girls.

*

Whenever we got bruises or scratches playing soccer or climbing trees, my father used to say that his mother used to say it was a good thing you could *see* the damage. It was when you couldn't see it, when something was wrong *inside*, that's when you had a real problem. I don't know whether he intended this to mean broken bones, or whether this was his oblique way of referring to the landscape of the emotional.

What I do know is that as soon as anything so much as touched on the emotional, it felt like we had strayed into the territory of the taboo. Another thing firmly in this territory was my mother's tears. (My father was not one to give advice, but I remember him telling me directly, when I was a girl becoming a woman, that 'if there's one thing men can't stand, it's when women cry'.) Countless mealtimes throughout my childhood I remember her sitting there sobbing, the rest of us pleading with her to stop. Whole afternoons on the weekend while my father was at work I remember her alone in her room crying with the door closed, my baking elaborate cakes in some attempt at consolation (in response sometimes she would be effusive with praise; other times she'd snap that I could have made dinner for once instead of all these bloody cakes). Trips to the supermarket when she would wear sunglasses to conceal the fact she'd been crying – chemist sunglasses (she was always losing them) with those ugly Polaroid side panels, which were supposed to be extra protection, though I wondered as a child whether they were protection from the sun or from others' gazes.

I eavesdropped on all my parents' conversations; 'He's like another person,' my mum would say about my dad when he called his siblings in France, so animated and exuberant did he sound. I would listen out especially to how he described me: even though he never expressed any kind of pride to our faces, over the phone his fierce pride of my sister and me was revealed, and felt more authentic for being delivered to me so obliquely. Once, in one of those curious moments that has lodged in me, I remember him answering the obligatory set of questions about how we each were, and when it came to my mother, these were his words: 'Tu sais, toujours pessimiste' (you know, pessimistic as always). As a child, this comment – the mean reductiveness of it – hurt me; I had never conceived of my mother in this way, felt a rush of defensiveness towards her.

Since my dad had always spoken to me and my sister in French, I assumed that I had a decent vocabulary. It was only in late high school, when I studied French formally, that I came to notice the curious gaps in my knowledge. *Chiante; fatiguante; emmerdante:* these words he would use freely, the same adjectives to describe my mother as to describe when the cats were fighting, or had knocked something over. But I had never heard the words *déprimé* or *anxieux* or *stressé* in any context. In my father's rural-nineteen-fifties-working-class lexicon, these words didn't exist.

Strange, now, to think of these holes in our language rendering certain things invisible, so that my sister's arms; my ravaged scalp; my mother's tears – they each joined the collection of things that we silently agreed not to speak about, and so we carried on, each of these things continuing to hide in plain sight.

In the same way he learned to hold my hands but not to look at them, my first boyfriend learned, without me ever needing to ask him, to avoid touching my hair. Our first year together, fresh out of high school, we spent inordinate amounts of time together, commuting to the same uni, where we were taking the same degree, sleeping at his mum's, his dad's, and my parents' by turn. But such was my determination to keep my secret from him, that even sleeping by his side I was not safe. On waking, my first instinct was never to reach for him, but rather to reach for my hair and check its arrangement was intact, and when it wasn't I would swiftly fix things, relieved anew not to have been exposed.

That first year, he didn't seem to notice anything unusual; I don't know whether this was the result of his male obliviousness, or his absentminded-professor personality, or my own hypervigilance. Whatever the reason, I sometimes lapsed into a kind of denial: that if he hadn't noticed, then surely the damage I'd done wasn't all *that* bad. (Though I also remember us bumping into people from our high school, how on more than one occasion they addressed only him, even though I was right *there*, so silent and vacant had I become.) In our second year together, the second year of our studies, and the year we moved into a share-house where we shared an enormous room, one morning he woke before me, said that while I was sleeping he noticed my hair 'looked funny'. I said I would tell him about it, just to give me a few days.

The first thing he expressed was great relief: he had worried that I had some kind of 'terminal illness or something'. He was tender as could be but even with the fortune of being with someone like him who *would* listen, I remained obstinate, convinced that my secret was too nebulous to even attempt putting into words; something the darkness and depth and hold of which was too large to be relayed or believed. He told me that he bit at the skin on his knuckles when he got stressed, and in my silence I let him believe that the two were comparable. I remember if ever I complained of period cramps he'd say he wished there was some kind of tablet he could take, so that he could experience the pain for himself. It's easy to dismiss this, now, as typical male inability to accept female testimony at face value, but I think it also reveals a stab at empathy, and awareness of a deeper truth: that pain is, ultimately, untranslatable. A few days later, he told me that he tried it – pulling out his own hair – and that it *hurt*.

From the cat protection society op-shop near our house he bought me a gift: several pairs of gloves, the elegant, embroidered kind. They were designed for women of the past with their tiny hands, but I'd squeeze my fingers into the least tiny pair anyway and wear them when he was around to let him think he had been helpful.

So he was the first person in the world to know my secret, or at least to know *of* it, but still he didn't half-understand its gravity. I don't mean that in a teenage, angsty nobody-understands-my-pain way. I mean that my secret felt so inexpressible and surreal and I didn't know how to convey any of that. And so we treated it like an unusual scar, the origin of which, once revealed, doesn't warrant repeating or returning to. Like a throat lozenge that can be tucked under the tongue, I kept my secret. Sucked at it discreetly; no one needed know its presence and I lived in hope that if I did this long enough, then eventually it would have to dissolve, and disappear, and nobody would ever need to know it had existed.

I was naive, of course.

I have come, these past few years, to spend a great deal of time in cafes, where there is little obligation to interact with anyone, and yet where I am able to be in the vicinity of other people, feel their eyes on me.

How I must look to another: a slight hunch in my back. In my right hand, a pen hovering over my notebook, my left elbow on the table, my ring finger shoved in my mouth (protective, intent, focused as a dog gnawing on a bone) a good centimetre deeper than a normal person would hold it to chew on their nail. And my expression so intense, looking straight ahead of me, but vacant, my eyes widened a bit. If I looked at someone's face like I am looking at the air, they would call it a 'death stare', I reckon. My legs crossed so that – unconsciously – my body takes up as compact a space as possible.

But oh, the great chasm between how I appeared to the world, and how it appeared to me! For in my experience, life is never unremittingly anything, and so even in those days where my compulsions consumed me, still the world let me glimpse her beauty; a beauty that helped, even if only momentarily, to lift me out of myself.

'Stop *staring*,' M will remind me, when he is with me, but when he isn't then I feel as though I could sit and watch people all day. The tiniest ones, two-ish, are my favourite.

In one of the spacious places not far from my home, music-less and therefore all the better for eavesdropping, there is one who loves to be plucked from her pram and, because there are no baby chairs, she gets sat on a stool, surveying her surrounds like she's perched high up in a treehouse. Remember when stools were something thrilling? Then there is the little girl who I have watched since she was still at her mother's breast, who has now learned to drink milk from a glass – a *glass* glass – and you can see how managing its weight, and tipping it at just the right angle absorbs her entire concentration, how proud she is of her new skill ... and it reminds you – the adult – of how much she has before her, to learn. After finishing her milk she migrates to the floor with a serviette, which she opens out like origami paper and then re-folds in different ways, lining up the corners perfectly, and then unfolding, and then standing, holding it out, like a parachute, and watching it dance its way back down to the floor. And another, a not-yet-talking one. His dad hand-feeds him bits of roasted carrot, and then he returns the favour, as though this is the way to eat, to press food into other people's mouths, not realising, I suppose, that he is only what we call a 'baby'. When they leave, he waves goodbye to me and to each of the staff in turn, and to the wooden table he has been sitting at, and to the pigeon just outside the entrance, and then to the bus whizzing past ...

I imagine, if those children were my own, my fatigue and my frazzled-ness would blind me to their miracle, or at least dim it, and so I feel inordinately grateful to be in their presence, a presence I haven't done anything to deserve.

In some ways I am grateful for my shame, too, for its power; it means that being in public can provide a kind of protection, for I am forced to step out of myself; to see myself from the outside.

When it's with me – the desire to pull, I mean – it's everything. I wonder if the phrase 'as soon as you turn your back' was invented for people like me. Sometimes I'll be in a cafe, head cocked to one side so that I'm looking straight at one of the only other people in the room, checking that her attention stays on her laptop or crossword or whatever, while I end up, surreptitiously, relinquishing. If she lifts her gaze (maybe because she can feel me staring fixedly at her) then I'll be able to stop at the last second and avoid being 'caught'. In these scenarios, my entire attention narrowed down to a flicker of movement, I feel savage, reduced to something animal.

The few occasions when I've suspected someone has actually witnessed what it is I'm doing, the shame has been so acute that the memory has lodged in me like a burr. I remember one especially intense episode last winter, pulling every half-line of my journal, holding each rooted one between my left thumb and forefinger in my lap, so that I could examine its appearance. The electric heater I'd positioned myself under was enough to heat my head and soften the roots, make them slimy. The tabletop was marble and when I let each root rest on its surface, it flexed easily around on itself, like a leech. Between my fingers, I held each just below the table edge, over my lap, so as not to be visible to the waitstaff or to the barista. I swear the waiter must have thought I was checking him out, must have wondered why I'd be into a buff guy barely in his twenties with his pulled-up socks and backwards cap, this anxious, not-so-young-anymore woman with her hair in an outdated bun. How to explain: I'm only watching to see that he isn't watching me, or more specifically, that he isn't able to see that I am threading a root of my own hair through my teeth. I swear I could feel the electricity coursing through my fingers, the little vibrations you might feel holding a sparkler between two fingers, or when you're hand-fishing and you can sense the nibbling, before the definite bite. And at one point I saw the face of the barista – maybe a metre from me – staring. Did he see? Or did he just have a fixed expression of slight aggression? Years ago I would have vowed never to return to that cafe again, out of shame. But it seems I've built up a tolerance – to shame, I mean. Is this what it means to be growing up? To strip your hair of its roots with your unbrushed teeth, and not to be mortified if someone sees you doing it?

Often, though, what ends up happening when I know I have no choice but to pull is to retreat to the bathroom. The good thing about a lot of cafes is they only have a single cubicle, which imposes a limit of sorts to my frenzies, because of course it would be only a matter of time before another customer came along and wanted to use the toilet. Several cubicles was a riskier prospect; it meant I could get trapped in there with nobody to interrupt me (or, as I had come to think of it, rescue me). So as a precaution I'd leave the door slightly ajar so that if someone came in they might think it was empty and push the door. If I heard footsteps I'd have to use a hand or a foot against the door to keep it from opening, a movement that was sometimes enough to interrupt the chain of my pulling. Another little trick I had (at least in theory) was to use the men's instead, since it invariably stank in a way that women's don't, and so, I figured, I'd be less likely to want to stay there. In these moments, listening intently to the streams of urine, followed by the little silence of unwashed hands, I felt freakish. I'd imagine what someone (anyone) would think if they could see me now: hunched over on the toilet seat not really designed to be sat on for such lengths of time, so that the sections of my body pressed against it went tingly; my lower back aching from the position (usually I had such good posture), my knickers hammocked around my knees, my bare thighs strewn in hairs; my un-muscled arms sore from being raised too long, and my index finger on my left hand invisibly marked from where I had run hair shaft after hair shaft, so tender that it felt with each new hair extracted that I was running paper through the slice of a paper-cut.

I wondered, too, who would find my aftermath – the intricate forest floor of dark part-curls – and what they would conclude, how puzzled or disgusted they would be. Usually the thought of someone seeing me leave the cubicle, and then seeing the hair, and connecting the two, was enough to motivate me to do a harried clean-up with bunched-up toilet paper, but sometimes all of me was spent.

This is what horror looks like: spending two hours in a public bathroom, listening to person after person try the latch, and eventually, having a cleaner do the same. It is hearing your own voice call out, in false brightness: 'Sorry, just a minute', legs gone to sleep, neck stiff, then stumbling out, just like when you stumble out of a cinema into the glare of the day.

I tried not to think about what waitresses might make of these prolonged disappearances. Despite ostensibly going to cafes for the protection against pulling they offered, some deeper part of me deliberately chose cafes that were large and bustling enough that my periodic vanishing might go unnoticed; I found myself returning to one place in particular where there was a high turnover of mercifully inattentive waitresses. I also made sure to choose seats that were tucked in a corner, my back to no-one. To this day, when a train is pulling in to the station, instinctively I scan each carriage to see if there are any seats at the very far end – not all carriages have them (just the old ones?) – just a single-seater, a little alcove because there's wall on either side, so nobody can see you from behind nor from either side. If that's not available then I sit as far towards the back of the carriage as possible. It's astonishing the number of people who are good as blind – absorbed in screens or with headphones, so that I register them as 'safe'. (The dangerous ones are children, who can be too alert for my liking.)

I come to hate the feeling when I emerge from a room (or

a bathroom) having pulled. I act all breezy, but I know I must surely be giving something away – can't you see it in the way I walk, or in my eyes? I feel conspicuously changed; altered; people must wonder what grave news I've just received. Or else they must assume I'm *on* something. My gaze lands on people and things too long.

Once on a train I remember having one of those six-seaters all to myself; the carriage filled up, but nobody sat near me. They kept on moving to other parts of the carriage, like I've seen people do when someone is obviously intoxicated or mentally unstable, or when there's a couple making out. I was not pulling when they walked past me – I am not shameless – but it was something in my composure that alerted them, perhaps, like you can sense someone on public transport is a bit *funny* without them having to do anything overtly unusual.

Unbeknownst to them, the women around me are classified, in my mind, as one of two things: threatening or colluding. Even though none of them knows my secret, has ever even attempted to pry. If someone has her hair tied back, I imagine she has done so out of sensitivity towards me. Tied-back hair is safer because it attracts far less attention, as a rule. I had a colleague whose hair was noticeably thinning along the part, and this made me feel uncharacteristically safe in her presence. People were unlikely to comment on her hair, and she was unlikely to comment on mine, either because she might guess at my self-consciousness, or because she wouldn't want any remark or inquiry to be returned to her, placing her in the spotlight. If I meet a friend and she has her hair out, I assume she is flaunting her un-bobby-pinned unelasticked hair. Or at least that she's been tactless. In any case, it's unsettling.

I've come to see the world as split into two kinds of people: those who pull out their hair, and those who don't. I imagine a line between us, which I have crossed, and which I am always wishing to re-cross, so that I might be able to resume my life, and be returned to the world.

# SHAME

I hate my stupid hairstyle, if you can even call it that. Hate this tightly fixed bun, which makes me look prudish, or as though I belong to another era. I don't like my (too-muscular) calf muscles either, nor my (slightly pudgy) stomach, nor the dark moles that are scattered on my face and neck, and that I don't usually pay much heed to, except that children like to point them out, one by one, and ask what they are, or even *why* they are there. But none of these possess the power that my hair does: to make me feel such bottomless shame.

When I pass a girl whose head of hair looks something like how I imagine mine would look if it were still to exist, I get a physical longing; a quickening in the gut. I'm envious of girls with beautiful hair displayed for all to see; the ease with which I imagine they and their hair glide through the world. I'm envious even of men with shaven heads, whose absence of hair does not lead people to believe they are cancer patients or Buddhist nuns or feminazis in the way that women's hairless heads do. At the swimming pool on my teaching prac, getting the kids ready for their lessons by retying ponytails; replaiting plaits; tucking loose strands of hair up into rubber swimming caps, I can't resist letting each girl's hair sit in my hands just a second, just to feel the weight of what I lack (and then I feel like a total creep).

It is a cliche that straight-haired women long for curls, and curly-haired go to great lengths to straighten their hair, and no-one much seems content with the colour nature has given them ... but my envy is a different hue: not so much wanting what others have, but wanting to reclaim what is rightly *mine*. I wish for hair of any colour or thickness or curl ... just anything longer than the sparse spikes that currently cover most of my scalp. I fantasise about how it would look if I managed to grow it even three centimetres, how it would feel to run my fingers through it. And what if I managed to get it a bit longer, so that it had some curl to it?

I hate that the fastidious arrangement of my hair fails to convey who I am, and what kind of hairstyle I would choose for myself if I had that freedom. At the same time my hairstyle exposes things about me that I would prefer not to advertise: that I am uptight; old-fashioned; unadventurous. But this disguise is preferable to the real (natural?) state of my head, which I would never expose in public. I don't know, any more, what the 'natural' state of my scalp is. Patchy and mutilated, or thick with the ghost-hair that only I can see in my own mind's eye?

*

If only hair did not *mean* so very much. What other part of the body could get labelled *untamed; feral; daggy; skanky; sleek; professional*? On shampoo labels: *damaged*; *breakage-prone* or, my personal favourite: *normal*. What other part of the body could we use as shorthand for an entire person: *curly top; carrot top; blondie; baldie*. What else could reveal age; epoch; wealth; ethnicity; sexuality; style; sickness; state of mind?

Hair is the repository for Mnemosyne's remarkable memory; it is the source of Samson's supernatural strength; it is Rapunzel's youth, beauty, and fertility. Virginal girls in Ancient Greece, on getting married, would cut their long hair and gift it to their goddess of fertility. In late eighteenth-century Western Europe, wealthy women spent hours having their hair arranged into elaborate designs (towering ships; birdcages). Such styles required maids to construct and maintain, and incapacitated a woman for work, and thus were evidence of wealth and leisure. In Victorian times, bereaved family members would keep locks of hair from deceased children or family members. These heirlooms were passed down through the generations, in lockets, small jars, plaited or tied with a ribbon, and sometimes sewn into the pages of books.

Until I began to read about the historical significance of hair, I wasn't really aware of the specific cultural practices associated with it. And yet, at some level, the various beliefs made sense to me. For within each of us lies a repository of all the fairy tales and stories and songs we've ever heard. And don't these, accumulated, create patterns, that we subconsciously use to read the world? I find the stories of malefactors and heirlooms and biblical figures oddly comforting, all these humans whispering across the centuries, 'Yes yes, we know: hair is more than hair'. It is spirit, seduction, strength.

In my own inner suburb of Sydney, nobody offers their cut locks to goddesses or sculpts their hair into birdcage designs, though to be fair, it wouldn't surprise me if they did. It's the kind of place where people eschew 'mainstream' fashions.

Nonetheless, there is hair symbolism galore here, too. I know that the mullets worn by the teenage boys who hang out smoking at the train station mean differently to the (ironic) mullet of my barista (and differently again, on a woman). If I pass a man with a full beard, I automatically read him as either Greek Orthodox, or possibly sleeping rough, or (if paired with a topknot) likely very into craft beer. A semi-famous writer whom I occasionally spot in the supermarket buzz-cuts the sides of her black hair, but leaves a small ponytail's worth longer, spouting from the very top of her head, and this identifies her as free-thinking, quirky, and politically progressive.

In retrospect, when I was teaching asylum seekers in detention, I think part of why I felt so uncannily at ease among my (male, Afghani, Muslim) students was that they were unable to read my hair, and by extension unable to read *me*. The hair that in Sydney marked me as outdated, uptight, and frumpy couldn't be read this way by these men, some of whom had never in their lives seen a woman in public with unveiled hair. To them, my brown, uncovered hair was unfamiliar, and unmistakably Western, a complete departure from their own standards of modesty and femininity.

I would dearly love to divest hair of all symbolism, but I can't help reading my own idiosyncratic meanings into the hair of those around me. Perhaps not the magazine-prescribed way, but meaning all the same. If a woman has too many blond highlights, or anything too obviously artificial, I find it off-putting, find I can't really take her seriously. A raven-haired young woman who lives on my street and wears her hair loose and un-styled has noticeable white hairs, which she never dyes, and for this reason alone I gather she has an artistic temperament, and is probably well-read.

And I find different degrees of hairiness and hairlessness evocative. I don't find full beards attractive at all, but then I also can't stand when my boyfriend is too cleanly shaven, and plead with him not to shave as often as he does. I find the thought of women removing *all* their body hair slightly creepy ... but then there's a woman at yoga with a very slight beard and I find her intriguing and have to keep myself from staring. I'm not very vigilant about shaving my own legs, but fortunately my leg hairs are not very coarse or dark, so I don't think twice about baring them in public. But if I see a woman with legs hairier than mine (especially if the thickness extends up to the thighs) I am taken aback at her bravado. It's not only a human thing either: I love cats, but only short-haired ones — I find long-haired ones ridiculous, and those sphinxy hairless ones make me recoil.

*

The ceremony of tonsure, in which portions of hair are removed from the scalp, is performed in several different religious orders. Here, the cutting of hair signals a novitiate's commitment to a life of devotion to God, and renouncement of their sexuality. In a Roman tonsure, for example, the whole scalp is shorn except for a rim of hair about the temples.

The so-called Roman pattern is shamefully familiar to me, since it so obviously resembles the design that has resulted from my fingers having pulled out so very much of my hair. Familiar to me, too, are the concepts of devotion and renouncement. I have often wondered whether the undesirable way I keep my hair marks me as having renounced my femininity altogether, renounced what might remain of my youth, renounced any chance at worldly beauty. Pulling as unwaveringly (as *religiously*) as I do remains the only reliable path I know to enter that expansive, timeless space; the only way to approach what some would surely call the divine.

'It's very you,' I have heard people say, to compliment someone's new style, and 'It's just not me,' when they're convinced a particular cut or colour doesn't suit them.

In *Shame & Glory: a sociology of hair*, Anthony Synnott contrasts what he calls hair's 'static' nature in more traditional societies (where it symbolises status and marks rites of passage) with its 'fluid' nature in the West, where changes in hair are rapid and ubiquitous. I thought, when I read this, of an aunt of mine in France, who, as we sat flicking through old photo albums, kept pointing out another of my aunts: 'See? She's had the same haircut for ten years!' Her meaning clear: how staid, how stuck-in-the-past, how *embarrassing*! I thought, too, of a (naturally blond, frizzy-haired) woman who worked in Admin at Curtin Detention Centre, how we used to refer to her as 'that eighties Hairstyle Lady'.

Perhaps it's hair's malleability that makes women insert it into conversation as often as they do. As early as primary school, I remember it being the standard way for girls to greet one another in the mornings: to coo at the choice of butterfly clips and glitter; to be scolded for braiding one another's hair in class; and to quiz one another about shampoo brands used.

At the English teaching college in Manly where I once taught, a coworker of mine goes for a dip in the ocean in her lunch break and when she's about to head to class asks us if she looks okay; she's worried that with her wet hair she looks like a 'drowned rat'. Another, who has the loveliest bounciest of curls – what the others call 'princess hair' – turns up one day with her hair straightened and later I overhear someone saying: 'I didn't *recognise* her. Not that one was better or worse ... she just ... she looked like another person.' Yet someone else fishes for compliments about her own new style: she's worried there's a 'very fine line between a cool-girl bob and a Mum haircut'. The sole male in the room laughs: 'But you *are* a mum!'

There are so many unspoken rules to all this to-and-fro; agreement to remark on certain things and not on others; different standards used to talk about others and to criticise oneself (imagine telling someone else they looked like a drowned rat! Imagine describing your own hair as princess-like!) People's failure to ever comment or ask me about my hair means I'm never clear about whether they have noticed its obvious patchiness, or what they have surmised. And so I feel hypervigilant, or deceptive, or inexplicable. Hair is currency, and hair is solidarity. I don't ever risk participating in any of it; I exclude myself and then end up being excluded in turn.

Lee Kofman in her book *Imperfect* interrogates our modern, Western inclination, to 'see the body as Other: a vessel carrying its commander, which we call a soul, or self, or mind'. Kofman writes about her own disfiguring scars, which, with her 'shell of stockings and long dresses' she goes to great lengths to conceal. Her scars make her feel 'not just ugly, but also profoundly different from everyone else, even *incomprehensible*'. As a result, she comes to suspect that 'the relationship between body and self goes both ways'; that 'beauty, as well as its supposed opposite, imperfection, can actually go deeper than skin, perhaps even to the core of us'.

Kofman's own predicament is, on the surface, quite different to my own – so, too, are those of the other people with 'imperfect bodies' she interviews to understand her experiences. And yet underneath our physical surfaces, so very much strikes a chord. Living such a guarded, uneasy existence can alter personality. One of Kofman's interviewees, the author Lucy Grealy (whose jaw cancer left her with some facial disfigurement), 'honed her self-consciousness into a torture device, sharp and efficient enough to last me the rest of my life'. Pretence and deceit can become part of one's makeup. Concealment, and the resultant vigilance for fear of being 'discovered' can take a toll so high it can 'shape one's soul'. Kofman says the places she has deliberately avoided 'have turned mythical'; the beach in particular has 'become a powerful metaphor for a certain abundant way of being'. My own equivalent place is probably a hair salon, which I have not set foot in this century. A place of beauty and glamour, of femininity and gossip and female communion. Each time I walk past such a place, I hold my breath to avoid inhaling the chemical smell, and avert my eyes, terrified that someone inside might see my terrible fear and longing.

Some compensate for their appearance by trying to behave 'perfectly'. Andy Jackson (who has Marfan syndrome) says he became tentative, cautious around other people 'as if I'm trying either to be invisible or to be seen as someone intelligent and caring – to be seen for personal, not physical qualities. Or perhaps the scoliosis has just intensified and complicated who I already was.'

In my own case, for periods, I avoided mirrors altogether, so that I could delude myself into thinking my hair wasn't all *that* bad, until on the rare occasion someone managed to photograph me, and it would invariably hurt me, to see how badly I'd fooled myself. To my mind, the state of my hair and of my nails completely obliterated all other facets of my appearance, and to compensate for this ugliness I needed to be exceptional – exceptionally good, exceptionally polite, exceptionally kind.

Attempts to transcend the body may also involve turning

to the worlds of art and intellect: I myself was labelled 'special' early on, and was, from the age of nine, separated from the 'mainstream', eventually earning HSC marks high enough to be offered a scholarship at a sandstone university, one that at the time looked (and felt) to me as enchanting a place as Hogwarts. The therapist I now see has more than once wondered out loud whether my pulling might be a way of holding on to this adolescent 'specialness'. I suspect that, subconsciously, it is – my education taught me to equate normality with lack. But because of the physical damage I've done in resisting normality, like Kofman I now need to outrun my body, which, in a strange circular way, has led back to me cultivating my bookishness and my writerliness, those traits that adults praised in me as a child.

After the publication of my first book, I remember how conversations would so often swivel back to my writing, which I became grateful for as a convenient stand-in for *me* – something to make me appear more successful and worldly than my actual embodied dishevelled self was ever able to convey.

Sometimes, instead of thinking my secret too large, I'm ashamed of its smallness. I fear the sadness and grief I swim in is not warranted in the way I imagine it would be if I had some other physical deformity because hair (putting aside all its symbolic value) serves no real practical *function*; it is superfluous.

Reading Kofman, though, I feel something like vindication, that my shame around how my hair looks is more complicated and not just evidence of my vapidity. Our zeitgeist, writes Kofman, is imbued with two contradictory ideas: that women have a duty to be beautiful *and* that they shouldn't be concerned with their appearance. Shamed for 'letting ourselves go' *and* for trying to improve our looks. She notes among psychologists a 'fashionable assumption that appearance-related sorrows are symptoms of erroneous thinking'. Yes! It is so very strange, this conspiracy to pretend that how we look doesn't matter one bit, at the same time as humans through history and across the world have understood that it *does*.

The result of this strange contradiction can be what Kofman calls 'vanity shame'. Embarking on the project of writing about her relationship with her body, she assumed the toughest disclosure would be the most obvious one: 'the public uncovering of my scars', but even more shameful than this, she realises, is her 'desire to look good'. (Her friend says scornfully: 'I never thought you were one of those ... women who worry about their looks.') My own shame around my hair was, similarly, twofold: that it made me look ugly, and that I cared about this fact in the first place.

Hair symbolism, writes Synnott, is 'usually voluntary rather than imposed or given'. But it may also be 'involuntarily imposed or expressed', as a form of subjugation or dehumanisation. Before being burned at the stake in 1431, for example, Joan of Arc's head was shaved (this is still a practice in US executions today). As for involuntary *expression*: 'The mad use their hair unwittingly.'

*

By this point, you'll no doubt have wondered why I didn't simply take a razor to my own scalp. As obvious a solution as this might strike you, I have never really entertained the prospect. First, having had the one hairstyle for a decade plus, it would, surely, require explanation to those around me. Second, it would make me look hideous. Third – and this may sound insane to you – some part of me knew that none of this was actually about *hair* per se. If I were deprived of hair to pull, I don't believe my need – for relief; for escape; for calm – would vanish, and I dreaded to think what other awful compulsion might take its place. The other thing is, I needed to believe that over time, however incrementally, I was making progress. Each individual hair still in place on my head represented such an enormous hard-won achievement; each was precisely where it was meant to be, and to remove them *intentionally* would have felt defeatist.

I couldn't help, reading Synnott's taxonomy of hair, trying to find where *I* slot in. I think I fell into the small subgroup of 'involuntary' cases, but was my own case 'imposed' or 'expressed'? I often felt as if it was imposed upon me by my own hands – was such a thing possible? One word of his stood out: *unwittingly*. Like an unwitting accomplice, I was implicated, but I hadn't *meant* to do the damage done.

Sometimes I wonder whether I have been cursed by this age, with its myths of individual agency and control; this delusion that we are each autonomous creatures, masters of our destinies. In the long years before I stepped foot in any doctor of the mind, I was convinced my problems were entirely self-inflicted. In another age, might I have been seen as possessed? Or cursed? Or just unfortunate? Might there be less onus on *me*?

'Hair not only symbolises the self but, in a very real sense, it *is* the self since it grows from and is part of the physical human body,' notes Synnott. Part of what it reveals about the self, in this strictly physical sense, is our health. In order to have lush, shiny hair you have to eat well, and, practically speaking, in order to look after long hair you have to have your needs in life taken care of.

In a malnourished person, whose protein sources are depleted, the body directs its energy to essential functions – organ function; retaining muscle tissue. Hair turns brittle and straw-like in appearance, and may stop growing altogether. When a person's eating improves after a bout of malnutrition, their hair actually sheds in large quantities – a sloughing off of the old, weakened stuff to make way for the new, healthier growth. Some believe this biological reality may underpin hair's symbolism. In the two years I spent teaching in detention, I saw young men visibly age as a result of their chronic stress and depression, and I remember, still, the hair of several turn from all-black to containing shocks of white.

I am generally acutely conscious of potentially damaging my body. I have never smoked; barely drink; never done drugs of any description; I have never even been tempted to get a tattoo. Part of me wonders whether I was compelled to pull my hair (rather than smoke weed, or overeat, or cut myself) because I think of hair as a superfluous thing. It can reveal damaged health, sure, but damaging *it* (eliminating it, even) does no harm to the inner workings of the body. It contains no nerves, and its only living portion is in the follicle. The visible part of the hair is, ultimately, dead.

I know there is a deep irony here: I have damaged the part of me that I deemed inconsequential, but in doing so have marked that which carries more symbolic weight than any other part of the body. I have chosen as the locus of my secret the part of me that is most visible to the world and most victim to its judgement.

As a child, I loved to dip a little paintbrush into an invisible ink of freshly squeezed lemon juice and write messages on paper, which later had to be held carefully above a flame to make the words appear. I only learned recently that this practice, of hiding a secret message in something that is not secret, has a name: steganography. Today, steganography has moved to the digital world, but the oldest documented case dates to 500BC: Histiaeus tattooed a message on the shaved head of one of his slaves, let the hair grow back, and then sent the slave to Aristagoras, who shaved the slave's head again to reveal the message.

Reading about the secret messages etched onto this slave's head, I thought, of course, about my own equivalent. My tightly fixed bun hiding the secret message right underneath it. The outward, unchanging appearance of my hair makes me look awkward, unplayful, and predictable (in turn solidifying my same inner qualities, in a vicious cycle). This masks the appearance of my scalp, which, if people could see it, and if they were told how it got to be that way, I feel sure they would find frightening. Evidence of my wrongness.

The secret I carry around on top of my head makes me feel devious; fraudulent; the gap between the person others see and the person I feel myself to be feels nothing less than a great chasm, and these two selves feel irreconcilable. I wonder how it would be to be someone like my sister, who has always had the ability to express her inner self through her outward appearance, who has marked her body in hand-drawn tattoos, for all the world to see.

When it came to my hair, there was also the issue of those pieces of it that were no longer attached to my body, that wove itself into my carpet, and turned up pressed between book-pages, weeks or months after having been removed from my body. A hair attached to a woman's head is beautiful, noted Mary Douglas, but the same hair that turns up in a bowl of soup is disgusting: 'Dirt', she famously declared, 'is matter out of place.'

While I was teaching in detention centres, the inescapable sense of surveillance put a lid on my urges. But after work, in my shipping-container room – unfilmed, unwatched – I would dissolve into nocturnal frenzies. It was a weekly cleaner who, concerned by the state of my room, took more than one colleague of mine (and eventually, my bosses) aside to ask: 'is she ... *okay*?' I think I'd kidded myself that my co-teachers found my general untidiness a source of amusement, or a sign of what they regarded as my eccentricity. But when my colleague passed on the cleaner's comments, I could tell he was embarrassed on my behalf. I felt exposed. I kicked myself for not having better protected my secret.

The bits of hair (the bits of *me*) that I left in my wake deepened my already-deep sense of shame and self-disgust. These bits of hair were dirty, and by extension, so was I. Why couldn't I leave my hair in its rightful place? If only I could do so, I might leave behind the feeling of never-quite-belonging; I might find a home away from my pulling; I might feel restored to my rightful place in the world.

Looking at herself in the mirror for the first time after a car accident that leaves her with facial scars, LaToya Jordan 'saw someone that was not the real me', and then she wondered, 'how would people know this wasn't the real me?' Kofman, after visiting a clinic to inquire about surgical options for scar removal, is left conflicted. She is no fan of scar metaphors, and yet: 'my scars have made some sense of me ... have anchored me ... even given me this pleasantly arrogant sense of being so unique that I'm *irreplaceable*. If my scars were barely visible, I kept wondering after the clinic's visit, would I be *me* at all?'

I have been asking Jordan's question for over a decade now: will people understand this isn't the real me? But when I've managed to, periodically, quell the pulling, I've been less aware of a sense of accomplishment or triumph and more of a profound sense of loss. Like Kofman's scars, my secret scalp has anchored me. The weirdness and wrongness of my rituals made manifest (if only to my eyes alone) the weirdness and wrongness that I believed was at my core. Imagine if I might start to look *normal*. Will I have destroyed what is most fundamental to my own sense of myself? What will remain of me?

I remember how at one stage when my hair was very bad, Chintz (one of our cats, the mother one) took to scratching out her own fur, until she ended up with ugly bald patches up her sides. 'She does it when she's stressed,' my sister would inform me, and she got taken to the vet, and bought expensive medication. Despite desperately needing not to be seen, at that moment I felt jealous of that rat-looking cat, that *her* hurt was visible, and tended to, and my identical damage was not.

# GOOGLE

Back when we were little, my father used to speak to me and my sister (his coquinettes) in French, and we were in the habit of replying in English, an arrangement that felt to all of us utterly natural. He himself had grown up in Alsace-Lorraine, mid-century; I remember flying into Paris with him for the first time in 1995, how people there would comment on how strong his accent was – it belonged not only to a separate region of France, but to another time. To me, though, his voice is accent-less.

In public, I was always secretly a little bit proud, that my father's words to us could be understood by my sister and me alone. (As an adult, though, I'm occasionally mortified at how inappropriate his observations about other people can be. His reflexive response to anyone he deems too emotional, or too large, or too needy, is to mock them. I have only ever encountered this attitude among people from his corner of the world. 'Lucky you're not famous,' my sister told him the other day, 'or you'd definitely be cancelled by now.' This made him laugh uproariously.) It always annoyed me that the French language should be considered so romantic and mellifluous, or that French people should be thought of as sophisticated, as these associations are so alien to me. For me the language is inseparable from my father. Inseparable, too, from the world of his boyhood, where his family kept rabbits and chickens and, he liked to tell us, his little brother would suck milk straight from the mother goat's teat. When a pig got slaughtered his uncle would shove a straw into its nostril to suck out the snot (the best part, my father said – still warm). In the winters of this world he used to stuff his boots with straw and newspaper. And his father would heat the car with a wood stove oven on the back seat, its chimney stuck out the window so the smoke wouldn't fill the car.

When my father speaks French he is not only more lively in spirit, but he feels more fully my father, if such a thing is possible.

Every six months or so, he'd take me and my sister on a Sunday train trip into the city. These trips consisted of browsing different bookshops, visiting Cyril's deli to stock up on (out-of-date and therefore properly ripe) Camembert and Brie, and then stopping near Town Hall on our way home for him to order a cappuccino, which he'd let me and my sister spoon the foam from, and which we all three considered the height of luxury.

Growing up, we didn't have much contact with other French people. But on these trips, when occasionally we'd happen to hear a random stranger speaking French, my sister and I would stop in our tracks, transfixed. Sometimes we'd even follow them around a bit, feeling as though we were spies, or had some secret power. It wasn't that we were especially interested in what they were communicating; it was that the words that we believed belonged to our father were coming out of another person's mouth. The effect was as disconcerting as if they were speaking in his voice.

This sense of ventriloquy and of utter transfixion is what I experienced when I learned that the strange rituals around my hair that I had long believed were my creation alone, were, in fact, a *thing*.

In the same way my father's vocabulary belonged to a language, my symptoms – though I had never conceived of them like that – belonged to what has been variously labelled a *mental condition*; a *psychiatric disorder*; a *rare disease*.

Annoyingly, I can't recall now how the thought came to me that maybe other people did something resembling what I did. What I do remember is in 2005, my second year of uni and my first year living out of home, I spent hours trawling the Fisher Library catalogue and eventually came across a book: *The boy who couldn't stop washing: the experience & treatment of obsessive-compulsive disorder*. Fisher back then was pre-ergonomic furniture, pre-microwaves, pre-sleep pods, pre-laptops. To retrieve a book I'd queue up for a computer on the ground level, carefully copy down the Dewey number onto the back of my hand, climb the endless spiral of fire-exit stairs, locate the correct aisle, and press the clunky light switch at the end of the narrow towering aisle, which would provide a window of light before you'd be thrown back into darkness without warning. This process sounds ridiculously convoluted, but I think at the time it made research feel thrilling, in the way of any hunt.

Written in 1989, each chapter of the book is devoted to a person (a 'sufferer') with a curious habit. One boy spends six hours a day washing himself and 'still can't believe he will ever be clean'; another woman can't stop checking she's turned her stove off properly; another can't stop plucking her eyebrows (it was this chapter, naturally, that I fixated on).

I remember loving that the book centred individual subjects and quoted their words directly. Re-reading it now, though (it takes me all of twenty seconds to download it onto GoogleBooks for $6.99), I am struck by the patronising and objectifying tone. 'Distinguished psychiatrist' Judith L. Rapoport MD is positioned as something of a detective in solving her clients' 'pointless rituals'. The book's blurb promises to reveal 'exciting breakthroughs in diagnosis ... and unravels the mysteries surrounding this irrational disorder'. The language – revealing; unravelling; solving – may as well be referring to murder cases.

To venture to even borrow the book felt exposing (I would have to hand it to a librarian to scan, and then carry it around on my person), and so I remember photocopying the relevant chapter, ridding myself of the original, and then secreting the copies somewhere in my bedroom in some corner or crevasse that was no doubt already dirtied with stray hairs.

Returning to the book now, some sixteen years later, I pity my younger self, who saw this book as an authority on the subject; an authority on *me*. Now, it strikes me as the literary equivalent of a freak show. It reminds me of that show *My Strange Addiction*, which my father and sister used to stay up late watching, and find totally hysterical. I was always early to bed, but the next day they'd tell me all about the woman addicted to eating mattresses; the man whose house was stuffed full with mannequins; the man who married a Ferris wheel. (Googling the show recently, I learned that there is an episode featuring a girl like me: 'Haley has been pulling her hair for over six years, but the big payoff for her is eating the follicle. Sometimes the hair-pulling can trap her in the bathroom for 2–3 hours a day, literally isolating her from the world.')

In the years since, several books have been published devoted exclusively to the topic of hair-pulling. I can't remember, now, in which of these I first learned that hair-pulling behaviour is most likely to begin in adolescence; or that it is more prevalent in females; or that those afflicted with this condition often exhibit other 'nervous habits', like nail-biting or jaw-clenching. I can't remember where I read that typically, people don't pull their hair around others; or that people often keep their symptoms to themselves.

I – who prided myself on being non-conformist – fit these descriptions as though cut from a template. Even the holes in my awareness appeared to confirm just what a stereotype I was: many people cannot identify any one event that appears to have precipitated their pulling. And it is not at all uncommon for people to be oblivious to the fact that their hair-pulling is in fact a condition (and not just their own weird quirk). Carrie, one of the women profiled in Dr Fred

Penzel's *The Hair-Pulling Problem* is typical in this regard: 'I was convinced I was a freak, and the sole person in the universe who pulled out their hair. Fear ran through me at times when I thought someone would discover my [pulling] and turn me into a guinea pig in the psychology labs'.

I have heard of other people with all manner of illnesses experiencing profound relief or comfort when provided with a diagnosis; a sense of things clicking into place.

This was not my own response: I felt robbed. In retrospect, I guess it was *I* who ought to have felt guilty of unwitting plagiarism, but instead I had the sensation that I had laboured nearly two years over an original work, only to have it reproduced and passed off as some stranger's creation.

So rattling was my discovery that for some time I remember my mind being in a weird kind of denial. I had believed so long that my compulsions were mine alone that part of me still wanted to claim the knowledge as mine. I had to keep on reminding myself that my habits existed outside of me. My illness defined so much of me, but I did not define it. It meant so very much to me but I meant nothing to it. It had its own completeness.

Wanting, I suppose, to reclaim my singularity, I decided that even if my condition might align to others' conditions in its generalities, surely how it manifested in *me* was unique. And in this uniqueness I might take solace.

Given this distancing impulse, in what I now think of as my first, most superficial harvest of information, it was all the variations of this condition that I zoomed in on.

People may pull from their scalp but also from their

eyelashes, eyebrows, beards, underarm hairs, legs and arms, and their pubic regions. Hair-pulling episodes can be short (lasting a few seconds or minutes) but occur frequently during the day, or they can be long (i.e. several hours) and occur less frequently; an individual's pulling tends to wax and wane in severity. Pulling may be confined to a specific area across time, or vary; the damage in these regions may vary from mild thinning to complete baldness. Some people pull in an 'automatic' way, where they are not aware of what they are doing; others in a more 'focused' way, where they are more overtly aware of pulling in response to a building tension.

But what was more rattling still was my gradual discovery – as over the following years I unearthed more and more information – that even the most weirdly *specific* aspects of my experience were not at all unique to me. Those who pull from their scalp (estimated to be some seventy per cent of pullers) do not pull in a design of their own choosing, but rather following an entirely predictable pattern and sequence: pulling almost always begins from the very crown of the head, and then progresses to the area around the ears. Pulling at the back of the head is generally an extension of pulling that starts at the top of the head. The hair growing from the nape of the neck is often left untouched, even by the most ravenous of pullers. I have seen illustrations drawn, which carve up the head into small, numbered sections 1 to 12, a bit like those diagrams of animals that you can find hanging in butcher shops.

This pattern of pulling mimics the male pattern of natural balding; it is also known as the 'tonsure' pattern. It startles me still, to do Google-image searches and to see a photo of a woman side-on, or from behind, who has pulled roughly the same amount of hair as me, and left an identical-looking border. The identical, triangular-shaped patch at the back of the head (with the crown as its apex), where the undesirable hairs seem to congregate.

I am scared that in describing these patterns to you I will come across as some kind of fanatic raving about crop circles, those strange patterns that appear mysteriously overnight in fields, provoking intrigue, and conjecture over who – or what – is responsible.

For my part, when I look at these women, I admit I do sometimes feel a kind of relief: that this was not all my own fault; all my own doing; that it was, at some level, beyond my control. A kind of *awe*, too, that we – these nameless faceless women and I, strangers to one another – have been swept up by the same implacable forces.

Those who pull often experience a deep sense of the 'wrongness' of their compulsions; when it comes to explaining how individual hairs are chosen, though, this feeling is reversed. Christina Pearson (who has made it her life's mission to create a community for those who pull) says the tips of her fingers 'tingle with electrical recognition when a proper hair is found' (note the passive voice: are her fingers the agent here or not?) 'It is as if I have struck gold when I find the right kind. Then, it must be removed. This does not come as a thought, it comes rather as a sense of rightness, a sense of knowingness'. The trance-like state that results is also a common experience. Dr Penzel, who has decades of experience treating compulsive hair-pullers, notes that many of his patients describe the discovery of pulling 'as if they had opened a door to another world'.

After pulling, individuals will very often engage in rituals, such as examining the hair, especially to determine whether the hair bulb is intact. Many report the pull is not 'right' unless the extracted hair has an intact root. Read enough firsthand descriptions of pulling and you will see a sort of hierarchy emerge, from the hairs that detach from the body with a calcified nub at the end, to those that have a black jellyish substance at the tip extending out a millimetre or so, to those that have accumulated a thin sleeve of grease around them, to those fattest ones of all, that combine black melanin, white root, and the rarest of all rarities: blood. And so many little rituals, that to the uninitiated must surely sound downright bizarre. Running the hair across the face or lips or tongue; holding the dark root up to the light to highlight the contrast between the hair shafting down the centre and its exterior shimmery part; dragging the root across paper to see evidence of its blackness; mincing the root with one's teeth. Anthony (another of Penzel's patients) describes his 'great concentration' in 'releasing the once buried little hairs': 'I find the thick hairs, some with their black sac still attached. I save those hairs like trophies, carefully laying them along the arm of the sofa, black against white.'

The eerie congruity of our physical compulsions is startling enough, but it is the congruity of our *interior* processes and patterns of thought that I find even more disconcerting:

When it begins, the conviction that you could stop if you really wanted.

And then, typically not long afterward, the feeling that you have no control over whatever this thing is. That is, a feeling that you have adopted this behaviour, but then the reality hitting you: that it – whatever this parasitical thing is – has adopted you; set up home in you.

The thoughts that plague you: that you must be crazy; that people would think you crazy if they knew. That you really ought to be able to stop; that your incapacity to stop is proof of your weakness; your inadequacy.

The decision early on to keep this thing hidden at all costs, and this compounding your isolation, your aloneness.

The gradual rearrangement of your life so as to avoid two things: situations that might fuel your pulling; and situations in which your secret might be discovered, so that the spaces where you feel safe come to feel narrower and narrower still. Mary Anne, who pulls her eyelashes and eyebrows, describes the lengths she goes to in order to keep her secret (reading her careful words, my heart is in my throat). 'I never let anyone stand to the left or right of me ... I tried not to look down, never closed my eyes in front of others, tried not to get my picture taken, and tried not to look anyone in the eye. I let my hair fall down my face and wore huge framed glasses instead of ones appropriate for my face size. Fear would rip through me whenever the topic of eyes came up ... I was in a constant state of fight or flight.'

And then there is the shame, so long nursed as wholly my own, but in fact a hallmark of this condition. Shame that means people avoid hairdressers, beaches, sport. Cynthia describes how as a child, she used to swim 'like a fish' but now, 'The rain and wind are my enemies. Water on a very thin-haired head shows everything. The brush of wind can move the few strands of hair that may be able to cover the bald spots.' I read about women who no longer leave the house; women who stop having sex; women who don't ever dream of entering into any kind of intimate relationship, such is their intense fear of being found out. I read of women who for years on end keep the secret from their husbands.

I was late to Spotify, as I am to most new technologies. Its *Discover Weekly* function impressed me. I had long assumed my own musical taste unreplicable and unpredictable (I mean, doesn't everyone these days describe their taste as 'eclectic'?) and so was taken aback by the disturbing accuracy of the algorithm to predict what I would like (and occasionally even to play some song that I hadn't heard since childhood, that my parents used to have on a cassette).

And with my pulling, it was as though all my little rituals – so much of my emotional landscape; the way I moved through the world; in short so much of *me* – was in fact beholden to an algorithm.

In each case, it was unnerving, that there should be threads imperceptible to me, connecting into a constellation things that I had assumed disparate.

(Though I suppose actually it was more like the reverse of a constellation, of the starry kind I mean. In a constellation, humans – in our hunger for meaning – connect together stars that in reality contain no path between them. We look at the sky and see gods and mythological creatures, chariots and telescopes.)

I had failed to see that my secrecy, my scalp, my sequences all formed part of the same architecture, and that this architecture was shared by others. I was like a bee so obsessed with collecting nectar that she forgot she was part of a colony. So fixated was I on my cell that I no longer saw the hive.

I, who saw pattern everywhere, who was in fact swallowed up by the intricate patterns of my pulling, had failed to see the larger design.

There is one thing more I have kept from you: the name of this larger design. The single word that encapsulates and reduces all the swathes of experience that I didn't know there were even words for.

Truth be told I have come to despise the word, so ugly, so clinical: *trichotillomania*.

From the Greek *trich* (hair) + *tillo* (pull) + *mania* (madness), the word was coined by French physician Hallopeau, the man credited with publishing the first medical report of hair-pulling in 1889. 'A bit of a mouthful,' I remember my first psychologist remarking. I never use the word, not even in my own head. I prefer to think of it as 'pulling'. Plainer, and more neatly contains the duality – the mental pull of the urge, and then the physical act itself.

I hate that this single word should signify so much about me; that it should collapse so much of my life – interior and exterior – into its seven syllables.

From the moment I discover this word, whenever I have access to a dictionary (especially the medical kind), I instinctively scour the T section. And then, when I land upon the space where it would appear (after 'trichiasis'; a condition where the eyelashes grow inwardly) a feeling of disappointment, followed quick on its heels by relief; that my secret is safe. Something thrilling to me, that the thing that most defines me, most people don't even know the *word* for, not even most dictionaries. For I am attached to this morsel of secret knowledge; to owning this word; to guarding this part of my identity that still feels to me the thing that is most particularly and privately myself.

One thing that bothers me is that I am unable to imagine inhabiting my disorder in any form other than its current manifestation. Despite the fierce urgency of my desires to pull out the hair from my scalp, for instance, I have never had the slightest inclination to remove the hair from my eyelashes or from my eyebrows (which, in fact, I plucked once as a teenager, and have never touched since for the pain). I am lazy when it comes to shaving my legs, especially in the wintertime, and yet not once have I even been tempted to extract one of these hairs.

It bothers me, that I cannot even *imagine* myself performing these behaviours so very close to those I already do; that I should flinch at the thought of removing an eyelash, or that the idea of pulling out a hair from my arm should strike me as foreign. Logically, my failure to imagine these things means that to someone outside my own strange constellations, my own actions must no doubt seem utterly alien; incomprehensible.

Similarly, when I learn that some people ingest the entire hair they pull (known as 'trichophagia'), I feel a total detachment (even, if I am honest, a morbid kind of fascination). I know, I know: I eat the roots – surely it is not such a stretch of the imagination to imagine eating the hair? And yet in my mind I think of the roots as distinct from the hair itself; a different substance altogether (as distinct as say a mango's skin is from its flesh) even though they are obviously parts of the whole.

If someone ingests enough hair, the compacted fibres – *trichobezoars* – can grow so large as to fill the entire hollow of the stomach. A kind of 'tail' extends into the small intestine. Over time, the build-up of ingested hair will form a rock-hard mass, which without surgical intervention can prove fatal. (In 2017, an outwardly 'bubbly' 16-year-old English girl fell ill at school; doctors failed to resuscitate her. The cause of death was found to be an infected hairball in her stomach, which had created an ulcer and led to her vital organs shutting down. Media reports referred to her 'Rapunzel Syndrome', a term coined for this phenomenon in 1968.)

In other species (gazelles, antelope, porcupines), bezoars are sphere-shaped, pearl-like deposits of calcium that accrete around bits of stone, made smooth by muscle contractions. Once upon a time, these intestinal obstructions were believed to possess mystical powers. They were incorporated into prized jewels, and ground down and ingested, employed as an antidote to poisoning.

Crazy to me to think that in other creatures and in other times, bezoars were endowed with life-giving properties but that in humans, they can be deathly.

In the strange specifics of my own condition, I am thankful at least for one thing: that I have no desire to swallow the entire hair. Though sometimes, sickly, I find myself envious of such a desire: *Then I would be able to prove how life-threatening this thing is.* It would be solid evidence; doctors would cut me open and be able to see plainly just how sick and wrong I was.

Even the most cursory clinical descriptions of trichotillomania often include a section cataloguing the damage this condition can inflict on the body. With protracted pulling, the hair follicle can be damaged, resulting in textural changes to the hair: it might regrow coarser, or kinked. There can be lesions or wounds at the site of pulling, especially when tweezers are used. The scraping of hair between the teeth can lead to enamel erosion. Calluses and cuts can form on the fingers, and the repetitive act of pulling can fatigue the muscles, leading to carpal tunnel syndrome.

Often this section is headed something like 'medical complications' or 'medical implications', and 'medical' here seems to denote all that which is not inside one's head.

I find next to nothing written on the specifics of how this condition can distort one's thought patterns, so that they, too, become kinked, eroded, fatigued, tunneled.

How does trichotillomania begin? Let me count the (possible) ways. The very first articles on the condition (from the early twentieth century) had a strong psychoanalytical influence. These framed hair-pulling as representing an unconscious sexual conflict; a kind of castration, given that hair signifies physical beauty and seduction. In a behavioural model (which posits that all behaviours are acquired through conditioning), the habit gets established because it is immediately rewarding, and through repeated practice becomes an over-learned response. In other words, sufferers unwittingly train themselves to pull. Somewhat counterintuitively, the earlier the problem starts, the easier it is to treat. Later (adolescent) onset is more likely to become an entrenched habit and accompanied by other psychological problems, whereas early onset (as young as in babies) is more likely to be outgrown.

Many psychologists tie the condition to a history of family conflict or to unresolved trauma, and a small percentage of people are indeed able to pinpoint the onset of their illness to a clear trigger: a death in the family; parental divorce. The theory is that the nervous system searches for a way to cope in the midst of a chaotic or stressful environment, and pulling is a way of self-soothing. But some reject the idea that hair-pulling is symptomatic of any deeper issue and claim that the condition is more likely neurobiological (in the way of, say, epilepsy or Tourette's).

It is also possible that these different origins are intricately tied together, or that different factors contribute in different people. I myself am skeptical of any model that reduces such a complex and stubborn problem to a one-size-fits-all explanation (or treatment, for that matter). The 'biopsychosocial' model is helpful in this regard. Often depicted as a Venn diagram of three overlapping circles, this model looks at the interconnection between biology, psychology, and socio-environmental factors (it may be applied to all manner of illnesses – in fact the World Health Organization adopted it in 2002). In the case of trichotillomania, biological factors might include a genetic, inherited predisposition for this illness, specific regions of the brain, and chemicals such as serotonin. Psychological factors could involve low self-esteem, and poor coping mechanisms; social factors might include family relations and moral values.

Some studies show hyper-activity in frontal-basal ganglia pathways among hair-pullers, an area of the brain involved in executing inherited motor programs, usually dormant in humans, but that in animals include nest-building and food-hoarding and social-grooming. One of the more fascinating-slash-disturbing learnings of all my research is that forms of hair-pulling and skin-picking are well-documented in other species. Birds who are stressed will chew, bite, or pluck their own feathers; mice have been known to pull their own fur and that of their cage mates to the point of total baldness; and dogs and cats may lick their skin or bite at an area, removing fur until there are bald spots and damage to the skin. 'Barbering' is considered one of the most pervasive behavioural problems in single-caged non-human primates. The phenomenon has not been documented in animals living in their 'natural' environments, only when confined in artificial ones. For this reason, animal scientists have classified it as a 'maladaptive behaviour that relieves the intensity of distress resulting from chronic exposure to environmental stressors'.

By this reading, the thing that is so big a part of me, is as much animal as human. The singular thing that makes me feel like a creature freed is proof I am a creature caged.

In the year of my birth, trichotillomania did not officially exist. It was, in fact, completely absent from the first two editions of the DSM, only included in the revised third edition, in 1987. Here, it was categorised under the dubious heading *Impulse-Control Disorders Not Classified Elsewhere*, alongside pyromania, kleptomania, compulsive gambling, and something called 'intermittent explosive disorder' (apparently: sudden episodes of unwarranted anger). And then in the DSM V (2013) – the current edition – its diagnostic criteria were changed, and it was reclassified under *Obsessive-Compulsive and Related Disorders* (a category itself newly created for this edition; previously OCD had fallen under *Anxiety Disorders*). In this classification, trichotillomania is officially grouped with body dysmorphic disorder, hoarding disorder, and skin-picking. Some medical professionals challenge this latest classification, instead likening the disorder to a substance addiction; still others see it as a form of self-harm comparable to cutting or burning the skin. Others draw a connection to tics (since these, too, are performed without conscious effort), or to the kind of compulsive-repetitive stimming behaviours found among people on the autism spectrum.

In the same way that my attempts to get my head around this problem result in frustration and bewilderment, the condition also seems to resist the medical world's attempts to categorise it. An unfathomable, shapeshifting thing.

The compulsive sort of perfectionism in terms of locating hairs that are 'right' for pulling is one resemblance to classic OCD, as are the repetitive ritualistic behaviours performed once hairs are pulled. However there are important differences: hair-pulling typically has a strong sensory component that people find stimulating and satisfying (while taking place) whereas the compulsions performed in OCD are not pleasurable. People with OCD carry out their compulsions in order to prevent harm or escape negative consequences that their obsessions warn the sufferer about. While hair-pullers can spend a lot of time thinking about pulling, these thoughts have a different quality – those who pull do not believe something bad will happen if they fail to pull their hair.

Superficially, trichotillomania resembles self-harming behaviours (like cutting, burning, or punching oneself). But the function is markedly different: self-harm is generally intentionally designed to produce pain as a means of obtaining relief from a negative emotional state, whereas the intention of those who pull is not to hurt or punish themselves. The damage caused by hair-pulling is a *result*, but not a *goal*.

Some frame trichotillomania as an addiction, on account of pullers' repetitive engagement in something harmful despite being aware of its undesirable consequences, and a history of repeated (failed) attempts to stop. However, hair-pulling involves no 'substance': if there is a sense of intoxication or pleasure, it is contained to the moments in which an individual is actually pulling. There is something inherently autonomous about trichotillomania, too: the puller is entirely self-sufficient in a way the alcoholic, for example, is not.

On one level, the impulse to draw analogies to other illnesses makes perfect sense, in providing a point of reference to build understanding. But on another, it infuriates me.

In *The Hair-Pulling Problem* Fred Penzel asserts that of all the various psychological disorders, trichotillomania 'probably remains the most misunderstood and the most mistreated of all. It would also be safe to say that in no other disorder do so many suffer alone and in silence.' For those incapacitated by such an isolating illness, it seems to me an added cruelty not to seek to understand it on its own terms, and to lump it together with other, close-enough things.

When it comes to treatment, cognitive behavioural therapy (CBT) is widely considered the treatment of choice. Patients track their pulling; attempt to increase their awareness of their emotional and situational triggers. They then learn to substitute incompatible behaviours aimed at reversing the 'habit' of hair-pulling. Newer treatments incorporate the addition of acceptance and commitment therapy (ACT), which for trichotillomania involves learning to accept urges to pull rather than trying to control these internal experiences, as well as recognising that no individual can be reduced to a single trait (like pulling). Since pulling is often automatic and is a state where the body and conscious mind are in a state of conflict, mindfulness practices, which heighten self-awareness, are also recommended. Medications can include SSRIs (as are prescribed for anxiety and depression), opioid antagonists (pain blockers), lithium, mood stabilisers, and the amino acid, N-acetylcysteine.

But just as trichotillomania is elusive in its causes and in its classification, so too is its treatment. The first controlled trials only occurred relatively recently, and to date, no single method of treatment has ever produced long-term, consistent, and reproducible results.

When I first discovered that my illness had a name, I was hopeful that it was just a matter of time before someone would discover a treatment. Over time, that hope morphed into frustration and despair. But also, if I'm honest, I felt a kind of vindication: see? my illness *is* more complex and stubborn than can be believed. A challenge, too: imagine if I could solve this unsolvable problem of mine all by myself.

But now, more than a decade on, hope or patience or anger – all this feeling strikes me as futile. Even if a magic bullet were found tomorrow, I find it impossible to believe it would do much to remedy a case as severe and as entrenched as my own. Instead, I need to make do with the tools I have at my disposal, limited and unreliable as they may be.

There's another, sicker and greedier layer of feeling, too: of *relief*. Nobody – no professor, no psychiatrist – has the power to eradicate my compulsions. They are mine to keep.

Whenever I've been required to provide a potted medical history to GPs or specialists, I've used the medical name for my condition. On every single occasion I've been met with blank looks: some have asked me to explain the nature of the condition; more than one has requested the spelling, so that they could enter it into their Google search engine, and then turn to *me* to mansplain me its (latest) classification.

My own experience with individual medical professionals reflects a more widespread ignorance. This is strange, given the actual prevalence of the disease, which is estimated to affect around two per cent of the population (a rate higher than that of, say, schizophrenia or bipolar disorder).

Why is this? People of my kind not only suffer from our symptoms, but from the paradoxical fact that we are the 'perpetrators' of our injurious behaviour. This results in a reluctance to pursue treatment: the average sufferer waits eleven *years* before seeking help. I suspect the shame seemingly hardwired into those that pull mean that they rarely discuss their experience in much depth, even with medical professionals. And when described at a surface level, the condition can sound so laughably trivial that it is easy to imagine it being dismissed as benign.

Mental illnesses like depression or anxiety still have enormous stigma attached, but they *are* increasingly talked about. And 'scarier' conditions like schizophrenia, eating disorders, and personality disorders are gradually becoming more well-known (albeit still misunderstood). The world of hair-pulling is so shrouded in secrecy, though, that I am not sure it even merits the word 'stigma'. It's not so much that people have misconceptions about trichotillomania; more that they have no conception of it at all.

Despite this prevailing ignorance, hair-pulling behaviours have in fact been observed for several thousand years.

Hippocrates, born four and a half centuries before Christ, and often considered the father of medicine, advised doctors to routinely assess for hair-pulling among other symptoms, and described a case in which a woman at the height of her grief 'groped about, scratching and plucking out hair'. In literature both ancient and modern, references to hair-pulling abound in the context of emotional turmoil. In the Iliad, for example, when Agamemnon is grieving on Trojan plains 'whensoever to the ships he glanced and to the host of the Achaians, then rent he many a lock clean forth from his head'. In the Bible, Prophet Ezra, appalled at Israel's unfaithfulness, 'rent my garment and my mantle, and plucked off the hair of my head and of my beard'. Shakespeare's Romeo, in defence of his infatuation with Juliet, tells Friar Lawrence that he cannot understand his situation: were he too lovesick and banished 'then mightst thou speak, then mightst thou tear thy hair, And fall upon the ground, as I do now, Taking the measure of an unmade grave'. And here is Rochester, at the critical moment when he and Jane Eyre first confess their love for one another: 'Jane, be still; don't struggle so like a wild, frantic bird, that is rending its own plumage in its desperation.'

Because my own compulsions feel so socially unacceptable, I was surprised to learn that hair-pulling has also at times been culturally and socially sanctioned. Ancient Greeks tore or shaved their hair to lay on funeral piles. In the Somalian Issa tribe, new wives, following consummation, pluck out their husband's pubic and chin hair. And to this day among the monastic Jain sect in India, the practise of 'kaya klesh' – a rite in which every hair strand is pulled out until the head is bald – is intended to denote detachment from pain, as well as teach one not to ascribe importance to the physical self.

It is strange – comforting, too – to learn that this thing that is my window onto something spaceless and timeless, should have existed in other spaces and times.

Even more fascinating to me is this: that in our current age, though nobody talks about hair-pulling, colloquially we still routinely speak of 'tearing our hair out'. We use it as a metaphor, to convey our exasperation when trying to deal with a difficult situation, or to convey our worry, sadness, or mental pain. The metaphor no doubt originated from actual observable behaviour, but now the metaphorical has superseded the literal.

It jolts me every single time someone uses the expression: my secret right *there*, voiced.

Like so many other sad young women, I grew up thinking that my body did not quite look right. I know, now, that back then I was athletic and slender, but even so, I never saw a body of my size or shape represented in advertising or films or by mannequins.

But visiting art galleries, seeing Classical marble sculptures up close, I have often felt a shivery kind of recognition. I still remember one time coming across a particular statue of a young woman at the Art Gallery of NSW, which I liked to go to in the summer for its air conditioning. She carried a bit of weight on her stomach; her calves were at least twice as thick as her slender forearms; her back was not taut with muscle but showed slight pleats of skin; her breasts, despite her youth, were not completely pert (if she had not been made of stone, you could have easily held a pencil under each, which according to various things I'd read was the gold-standard test of assessing the need for a breast lift). In short, her body was as identical to mine as I had ever seen. It felt almost exposing, to have her there, naked, people looking at her from every which angle.

I remember M whispering: 'She looks like you.'

And I remember thinking: *She's so beautiful.*

And there was something weirdly beautiful, too, about the discovery that I seemed to have been made in the same image as this woman. Her flesh long gone, but her body mirrored in mine.

And a feeling identical to this came to me when I saw, for the first time, the act of hair-pulling rendered in stone. Circa 1660, the sculptor Artus Quellinus (I) carved a life-sized, sandstone statue of a woman pulling out her hair (which reached me via Google). Her posture is horribly contorted; her face, too. One hand grips half her hair and pulls it toward the ground; the other yanks the remaining half of her hair skyward, so that the hair ends up forming a single vertical axis. It is around this axis that the woman seems to revolve. Originally she stood in the garden of the Dolhuys, a municipal 'madhouse' in Holland, though now she lives in the Rijksmuseum where she has been named *Frenzy* and described as 'frenzy personified'.

In whose image was this sculpture made? Whoever she was, I felt a rush of recognition looking at her sculpted form.

In obvious ways she was very distant from me: we

belonged to different centuries and hemispheres. She was made of stone, and I was deprived even of her stone-flesh, only able to see her from one angle, on my laptop screen. And yet, I felt I knew her. I felt I understood something about her, and that she understood something about me. I find myself, still, returning to her image again and again, just to study her face, as though it were a newborn baby's. I can stare and stare at it; it brings me strange comfort, just to drink in her miracle and her mystery.

There is one final discovery I ought to mention. When I chance upon it, in 2015, it's with the thrill of a gold-panner having worked through litres of muck (or to use an analogy closer to my own experience: after discarding hundreds of unsatisfying strands of hair, finally unearthing one with its root attached: glistening and whole). It is a short story by Mexican writer Guadalupe Nettel, who was born in 1973, and is writing today. The narrator of 'Bezoar' addresses her correspondence to her therapist, Dr Murrillo. She discloses to him 'a habit you yourself couldn't imagine and, therefore, can't even attempt to cure'. Despite it being 'the origin of everything: the vice that begets all vices', she has never mentioned it to him before, since something in her wanted to 'preserve this one intimate space'.

Her habit is mine. She describes the morning when as a girl in front of her mother's bedroom mirror she first discovered the 'anatomy of a hair': the 'hidden, slimy part that makes up the root (that) provoked an animal aversion in me'. And her impulse to swallow the root: 'It came from inside my body, and so it only seemed natural to return it to the bottomless depths it had come from.' Now an adult, she returns to the ritual compulsively 'like someone seeking refuge in a magic spell'.

> It seems to have always been a part of me, as for an insect that can't help but taste the pistil of flowers that have attracted its species since the beginning of time. It will seem stupid to you, doctor, but during these moments I've come to believe in an eternal recurrence of past lives in which I also, inexorably, plucked out my hair.

Not once in the narrative does Nettel label her behaviour; in fact she doesn't even allude to the fact that it is anything other than her own idiosyncratic habit. Her pulling is, first and foremost *her intimate space*; nameless and unnameable. Which is exactly how I experience it, still.

In the copious amounts I have read on this subject over the years, I have always ultimately ended up feeling exposed or categorised or pathologised. But here, in the space of this story, I feel great kinship. Guadalupe Nettel is regarded as one of the greatest living Mexican writers. Her characters, writes Mariana Enriquez, 'inhabit bodies which are strange places, so much so that they lose their human form'. Reviews of Nettel's work invariably contain words like 'disquieting', 'perverse', 'disturbing'; she 'veers towards unknown and dark corridors'. And yet to me the Nettelian world feels uncannily familiar. For my own isolation and loneliness and otherness, her writing is a salve; my very own bezoar stone. I see that even if my story is like her story, is like so many other stories of secretive girls through history, still it is important, and precious, and profound.

Even in the most comprehensive discussions of trichotillomania, I am left with little sense of the heart of the disease. It is all cause and criteria and cure. No place for the sacred. No place for awe. No place for words like *magic* and *eternal* and *the beginning of time*.

# THE PIECE

In the decade that followed my discovery in 2005 that my affliction had a name, I read all the books and case studies and Reddits and blogs on the topic I could find. And whenever I came across mention of wigs and hairpieces, I was thankful at least for not having gone *that far* ...

I'd inspect the hair of every stranger in sight – its volume, its sheen, its bounce. I was alert to a lack of hairline, to anything suspiciously tidy, to the quick darting-adjusting gestures some women make to their hair when a train pulls into its stop, which are distinct from the subconscious fiddling movements of other women readying to present themselves to the world. And whenever I detected a wig or any kind of hair extension (or at least, believed I did) I couldn't help but feel a vicarious kind of embarrassment: did you really think you could get away with it?

And yet. In op-shops in those years, whenever I'd come across a tangle of wigs – the cheap, plasticky kind – my instinct was to stuff one into the sleeve of a random jumper or the leg of a pair of jeans, and sneak it into the change-room, to see what it looked like on. To be clear: I was not interested in disguise or makeover. In my new reflection I saw a person who better resembled the person I *should* look like: the original restored. She who was my past self and who I still believed my future self would resemble. And once removed, all I could see in the mirror, perched on top of my head, was the giant blank space of what was missing.

I suppose my resistance to wearing a wig was a denial of just how out-of-hand my problem had become. It was not only the physical damage I'd done that I was in denial about, but also my capacity to put an end to my pulling. I was forever making resolutions and calculations – that I would, on such and such a date, put an end to my bad habits once and for all. Even in those passages of time when I was completely under the spell of my urges, still then, part of me kept denying their power over me, always believing that if I *really* wanted to, I would be able to stop, surely.

To wear a wig would be admitting that my willpower was not enough. It would be proof that I was unable to deal emotionally with the world, such that I had to resort to pulling. For ages I'd believed my urges arose randomly and unpredictably, but they definitely intensified when I was upset, or stressed, or simply tired (as well as, inexplicably, whenever something happened to put me in an unusually good mood). Proof too, that I could not face the world physically either, and required a disguise to do so.

At some level, though, I must have been aware that I had

in fact already come *that far*. In the sealed space of the op-shop change-room cubicle, my denial was momentarily undone.

The loss of my hair was sufficiently gradual that – or so I managed to convince myself– as long as I was able to conceal the scalp, I was safe. By which I mean: my secret was safe. To start wearing a wig overnight would draw such sudden unwanted attention to me, would change my appearance so dramatically, that I would have no choice but to explain to those around me what had happened to my *actual* hair.

What was supposed to be the ultimate disguise would in my case be the ultimate exposure.

It was, of all things, a book – my own book, as a matter of fact – that was the catalyst for me to begin to look into cosmetic options. It was 2016 and my debut was on the verge of being published, and I didn't want to have to attend the obligatory launches and interviews – anxiety-inducing enough – and be preoccupied by the state of my hair. I remember a publicist telling me that if I did get asked to appear on telly (thank God I never did), that seeing as asylum seeker issues were something of a sensitive subject, I always had the option to 'go incognito'; that I could wear glasses and that it was 'quite amazing what a wig could do' ... had she seen my scalp, or was I being paranoid? Was this her tactful way of helping me in a way that didn't draw attention to the fact that she was doing so?

My decision was not a question of wanting to look nice. Rather, I wanted to be able to stop thinking about my hair altogether. Naively, I imagined if I forked out enough money, and if I was less ashamed of my appearance, then I'd experience a surge of confidence and my compulsions might resolve themselves. How I longed to be relieved of my hypervigilance; the feeling of always being on the edge of humiliation; the toll that this was taking.

By filling in the space where my hair ought to have been, I thought I would clear up an equally large space in my mind, so that instead of being consumed by paranoia and suspicion and calculation, that section of my mind could be filled with other, nobler preoccupations.

I didn't entirely know why I was googling, or even what to google ... but somehow I found a select few 'hair restoration' companies in Australia, only one of which, Transitions Hair, is in Sydney. Its recorded message advertises their products as 'natural, beautiful, and undetectable'. Of course it was the prospect of undetectability that lured me; as mythical-sounding as an invisibility cloak. Maybe because my sole desire was for my secret to be made invisible, I did not stop to visualise what the hair would look like, how it was going to actually *work*.

I ought to say, I am finding this hard to tell you, harder even than I anticipated. Maybe because I feel – still – so fraudulent about it all; like my compulsions already require so much duplicity, and this feels like an extra level of deception, that I have gotten away with (at least, I believe I have) until now.

What do I remember of that first visit? How when I

woke, M hadn't left the house yet, because he had decided to accompany me to the appointment, and how this was a big deal because his bosses at the time were dodgy and taking a day off or knocking off early just wasn't an option. (Whenever his boss would call, M would have to hold the receiver at a distance from his ear, such was the volume of his yelling.)

How upon entering the place, I felt the kind of edginess that I imagine a married man might feel visiting a brothel. We were ushered swiftly into a small waiting room of sorts, curtained off, not like at a doctor's where you wait alongside other patients. The layout of the place, I would come to understand, seemed to have been designed to prevent clients from ever needing to cross paths.

I remember, that very first visit, being impressed at how slick it all seemed. It would take several months' worth of visits for me to see that the giant orchids at reception were not, in fact, real, and that the generous piles of *National Geographic* magazines were several decades old. How hyper-alert I was. I couldn't help studying the owner's hair, a uniform strawberry blonde. Andrew, his name was. Was it really normal for a man in his forties to have such a full Tintin-like head of hair? In any other circumstances I would not have looked twice at this clean-cut man, let alone at his hairstyle, but now I studied it intently, determined to detect some sign of its fakeness.

I was alert, too, to his impression of my hair, though I didn't pick up so much as a flicker of the repulsion or intrigue or pity I'd expected to.

While we were waiting, I remember, we leafed through

the coffee table books showcasing all the options available. Charts showing gradating levels of damage, from a barely perceptible thinning along the part to more obvious loss. Everything here was classifiable, categorisable, medical-looking. Male patterns. Female patterns. But my own pattern wasn't on the diagram; my own negative space at least three times larger than the worst of the women depicted.

Another page had a close-up photograph of hair at its base. It surprised me, the way it grew. I'd pictured it like the way arm or leg hair grows— single hairs more or less evenly spaced – but in the photo there were multiple hairs sprouting from the same spot. Mostly the scalp skin looked very pale, but there were shadowy sections mottled through it, like shark-black blurs on an aerial photo of an ocean's surface. Were these the black roots submerged beneath the skin?

Andrew knew the word for my problem. I had seen it on his website. I had never heard anyone utter it before, and the dispassionate way in which he said it, as though it were a word like any other, made me trust him. He told me about another of his 'clients', a girl who he said had the same problem as I did, and this made me trust him, too – that he had even been in contact with someone like me, which I myself never had, and still haven't. (In a large city like mine, there are meet-ups and programs these days for all manner of afflictions but none for people like me. I sometimes found myself wishing I was an alcoholic, because anonymous meetings in basements would surely be preferable to being this alone.)

Andrew said when his client's mother saw her with her new hair for the first time, she burst into tears. (And this filled me with envy, that her mother should have been entrusted with her secret.)

I remember no other details of that girl's story now; all I recall is that at the end of it he allowed a pause to develop: 'You don't *have* to share your story if you don't want to.' I didn't know how to tell him that I didn't really know what my own story was.

He asked me what I was after; what *look* we were going for. That was probably the point I realised I was no longer able to stem the tears. I told him I didn't want a full wig – I didn't want anything fancy. All I wanted was to look 'presentable', by which I meant I wanted to be inconspicuous.

I don't remember how he framed his request to look at my hair, at what we were dealing with. I undid my meticulous arrangement for him, making him the second person on the planet to witness my scalp in this state: naked, and defenceless.

I could tell that he was taken aback at the damage I'd done. And I was ashamed, but also sickly proud, of my own extremity and my ability to conceal it.

He asked me why I was so averse to the prospect of a wig, indicating some enormous photos on the wall. They'd done the shoot in Bunnings, he said, and at some point someone – maybe the store manager? – had asked, what are you *actually* advertising? He'd been studying the models and couldn't work it out. Andrew told me this story, of course, as proof of just how good his products were. How convincing.

But the women in the photos had lustrous manes; femme-fatale hair. I didn't want that. I wanted him to help me fade into the background.

From the pristine chest of drawers behind him, he removed an example of a 'topette'. A pony-tail sized switch of hair, secured to a base roughly the size and shape of a Jewish skullcap. I suppose I'd imagined all the hair on display, like you see in African salons on high streets. But there was no hair in sight here, just so many compartments, inside each of which I imagined must lie a zip-locked bag of hair, like some kind of museum archive that required classification and care. It all felt so *illicit*.

He held the piece of hair out for me, so that I could hold it. This, he explained, could be attached to the crown of my head, hidden in amongst my own hair. The base was made of several layers of silk, designed to be able to breathe easily. Each individual strand of hair had been individually drawn through this silk net, and then knotted in on itself; a process apparently called 'ventilating'. It was the very best 'virgin hair', which, I learned, is not some kind of sacrificial offering, but simply hair that has not had any kind of chemical processing and that is collected from a single donor. 'Guaranteed European,' he assured me.

He passed it along to M, so that he could feel it, too, and I felt a surge of jealousy, that he so enjoyed the feel of someone else's hair running through his fingers.

I said my main concern, really, was the cost. He said he did have other pieces from India and from South America, but – in language that brought to mind nineteenth-century anthropologists – he said that they were inferior products: coarser, and not guaranteed to be virgin. (It wasn't unusual, he explained, for makers to combine hairs from various sources, not only from different humans, but from animals.) And there were less costly, synthetic options, but I'd end up disappointed – they would tangle too easily, and because they didn't have that natural sheen they wouldn't look 'as real'. The Russian products, like the one he'd shown me, were really far better, especially to get that lovely feeling of the wind through your hair.

It was strange, to hear him talk about hair as a material thing; a product.

He suggested I try on a few versions, warning me first that it was a bit like trying on a new dress, that it might look a bit funny – just like a hem might need adjusting, or a waist might need taking in, you needed to have a bit of imagination. Once I'd chosen a piece, he explained, I would have two options: either they could glue the piece directly onto my scalp (the glue in a ring around the edges of the piece), or they could use special metal clips. The advantage of the former was that it would feel more secure on my head, whereas the good thing about clips was that you could remove the piece when you were home, or when you went to bed (and as a result, it would only need replacing in around two years, rather than one). Either way, the piece would sit on the very crown of my head, my natural hair around it.

Glue, I told him, would probably be my preference, because that way my fingers wouldn't be able to reach my scalp, and that way hopefully my *actual* hair, sitting under the piece, could begin to regrow. He explained that I'd need to make ongoing monthly appointments, so that they could re-apply fresh glue, as well as give the piece a professional clean, and then tidy up my own hair as well.

They'd need to perm the hairpiece, so that it matched my own hair. And my own hair, he said with some sorrow, was quite 'ashen', but what they would do was dye my hair, to brighten it up a bit, because that was easier than trying to alter the piece too much.

When he turned to ask M's opinion, M beamed: 'It makes her look *amazing*!' And I hated him, because I looked utterly ridiculous.

The distinct shame I felt being here displaced my usual shame. Here, I felt shame at my own vanity. Shame at handing over enough money to buy a car (a small second-hand one, I mean). I tried not to dwell on the fact that my cloistered inner world had been turned into a transaction, a chain of people looping around the world profiting from my own failures. There was something icky about it all.

(Now, I see that I was conceiving of all this the wrong way round. I was apprehensive about being ripped off, but completely ignorant of the broader economic reality. In actuality, the women who donate their hair often do so out of financial necessity. In Peru, for example, hair merchants buy hair from poor women in village marketplaces, as a key source of income. There is long and tedious labour involved, too: hair processors must clean and sort and disinfect the hair. It takes a skilled wigmaker two weeks to assemble a full wig.)

I remember on the way out, how in the reception area where there were different products on display for sale, M picked up some kind of helmety electromagnetic contraption, supposed to reverse hair loss in men. He inquired about it, and

Andrew said it was effective in some ninety per cent of cases. I was skeptical, but M could be gullible when it came to these kind of gimmicks and gadgets. *That kind of fake*, I thought to myself, *wasn't at all the same as my fake*. My fake was real.

Two weeks later, once my new piece – that is what I come to call it, 'the piece' – was ready, Andrew held it up to compare it to my own hair. All I could think, now that it was curled, was how *much* of it there was. Next step was to dye my own hair. He kept ducking in and out of the room for different things and each time I found myself needing to pull, though each time he returned I tucked my hands back under the smock. All this was new to me because I'd basically never stepped foot in a hairdresser's in my life. I didn't know how something like hair-dye actually worked: the sludgy paste was smeared not only over my scalp but also over the skin of my upper forehead, and I wondered whether it might leave a temporary stain, or whether it contained something to make it only stick to hair and not skin?

To secure the piece to my head, he traced around its base with a pencil, directly onto my scalp, and then used an electric razor to shave that section, the idea being that this would allow the piece to sit as flush against my scalp as possible, and that the glue would stick better to skin than to an uneven mat of hair. He removed not more than a couple of centimetres of length, but still the reality of this shorn section was hideous, like a patch of just-plucked chicken flesh. I was glad M wasn't there to see it.

Then he used a little paintbrush to apply a border of glue, positioned the piece carefully, and pressed down to secure it. *Well, at least that section of my head is safe now*, I thought to myself, the glue forming a sort of locked perimeter fence. Protection from myself. Carefully, he arranged my actual hair, so as to conceal the edges of the piece.

He looked mighty proud of his work, at how well he'd managed to match the colour and the curl, even took some photos from different angles on his phone.

Out on the street, I remember, at the lights, this guy looked at me, the kind of guy who shamelessly checks out other women even when his girlfriend is right beside him. In other words, the kind of guy whose attention I would never usually attract. And while I felt something like victory, inside that feeling was another: that I'd tricked him, that I wasn't the kind of girl he thought I was.

For the first days of wearing the piece, I felt more self-conscious than ever. Each time I had to see someone, I was terrified they'd notice. I remember being most scared of all of meeting my sister – surely she of anyone would notice – but by some weird coincidence, for the first time in her life she had just shorn her head completely, and so all her attention was concentrated on her own scalp, on my assessment of her. This made me feel invisible, which is what I wanted, I know. But I remember it hurting, too.

I rarely thought about the woman whose hair I carried around with me, still. Maybe because I was typical of women of the West; oblivious to how the items we consumed were grown or sewn or manufactured. Maybe, too, because I'm used to it – to using other people's things, I mean. But it *is* strange, now I'm putting this down on paper, to think about the Siberian winds that might have ruffled this hair; who it might have seduced; the lover that might have caressed it ... And I wonder, too, if she ever stops to imagine the person now walking around with her hair upon their head, claiming it as their own?

Within a couple of appointments, my hypervigilance fades, and I settle into a new routine. I learn the train timetable (fifteen-minute intervals apart, which means I'm always ten minutes early and so I use that time to wander around the Vinnies downstairs from the clinic. Though sometimes I catch the train that arrives five minutes late in a deliberate attempt to disrupt my own punctual good-girl image). Each time I approach the building, walk through the foyer then the lift then the corridor, whoever I pass I scour for signs they are headed for the same place I am, and are therefore of my kind. The electronic door chime sounds, and I'm ushered into one of the vestibules by Annalise, the stylist assigned me by Andrew. She will offer me tea or coffee, which I invariably accept, partly out of politeness and partly out of some resentment at pouring so much money into this place that I want to get every dollar's worth I can.

While my coat's being whisked away, I un-pin the piece from its perch on my head, and sit it on the little ledge beneath the enormous mirror, so that when Annalise returns, both it and I are ready. A bit, I suppose, like the way a life-drawing model will undress behind a sheet even though seconds later she will appear stark naked. Something too intimate – erotic, almost – in the act of unclothing.

Then she will escort the piece into another room. The sound of a tap running, the easy chatter of other staff (who I come to know by voice alone) talking about their weekend plans.

It seems to me Annalise can sense my shame: even though I am walled off from anyone else, she talks to me in a loud whisper, leans in towards me slightly rather than ever speaking across the small room. Then she will direct me to the chair abutting the sink so that she can wash my hair. How to describe the sensation of water on scalp? So simple a thing, and yet something I never do in the presence of another (I will enter the ocean with a hat on, and avoid diving underwater; even showering in my own home, if someone other than M is there I never leave the bathroom with wet hair). How I like the sudden heat of it, the incomparable feel of water on skin. And then her bare fingers upon me, pressing into skin that is so used to being pulled against. It is almost too much. A different kind of surrender. I keep my eyes clamped shut, terrified of the intensity of feeling they might betray.

Over the years I have seen more than one doctor to get my skin checked for suspicious spots and moles. With the last one I had the feeling that when he examined my inner thigh he could have been looking at my elbow; the space in between my breasts was the same as a kneecap. His manner like he was opening an email, no betrayal that what he was looking at was my naked soft flesh. Annalise is not like that.

I don't know what streams through her in these silent moments. What must she think of me, who month after month returns to her with my strange, Sisyphean requests. It doesn't feel like repulsion, or surely I would be able to sense some kind of flinching in her fingertips? I need her to be tender and patient and sensitive, but not to pity me. Professional but not clinical. I need her to understand the gravity of my situation, but not to try to amend it.

These are all such fine lines, which I ask her, secretly, to tread.

After the shampoo she puts what she calls 'treatment'. I don't know what the substance is and don't care. Sometimes along the way she will clarify what she's doing, or outline some alternatives, but it feels superfluous, like when my bike mechanic might try to explain the repairs he's done.

And then it's done, and it feels so ... abrupt, so unceremonious. I shift to the other chair, in front of the mirror, and she will pull down the specially-made blind to cover it, because she understands that I find my reflection in this state unbearable.

Then she will leave me there, while she disappears to tend to the piece in another room. When she brings it back it will be like new, especially the underside, which looks grottier and grottier each time I hand it over. She will ask if I want a trim. The first time, I was paranoid about how much she would take off, and to this day, each time I will remind her to only take the bare minimum. I know this must seem illogical, to pull so greedily, and then to be so precious about some dry split ends ... But the hair that remains *is* so precious – it represents (if only to me alone) so much restraint, so much discipline, so much time. Once my hair is dry enough, she positions the piece on my head, checking with me that it's the right distance from my hairline (too close and it risks being visible, too far back and there'll be a slit of scalp visible).

Sometimes, in the pockets of time when she is not in the room, I will pull a little. I need to be on guard for her return, which is tricky because the doors here are soundless and my seat is positioned in such a way as to be visible as soon as the person opens the door. I have to be careful, too, not to touch the still-tacky glue. Whatever the treatment is seems to penetrate down and feed the roots themselves (is that possible? like thirsty little plants?) so that they seem newly engorged.

I am careful, though, to have a *Marie Claire* positioned on my lap so I can feign absorption in *it*. Then, a second application of glue. And then the piece positioned carefully, her weight pressed down through her hands to secure it. Then she will scoop my own hair back, scrunch something through it with her bare hands.

And then I will tie everything back myself, not actually caring about the hair, only that there is no evidence of the zone beneath it, devoid.

At this stage, I imagine other clients must make some sort of comment or pass some sort of judgement, but I never stop to admire her work or my appearance ... She is surprised, at first, at how unfussy I am; that I tell her each time not to bother about blow-drying my hair and that I don't want any style as such, don't even ever wear my hair out but keep it tied safely back.

Between my appointments, too, a predictable sequence develops. Its own monthly cycle.

For the first week or so, when the glue is fresh and the piece is un-budgeable, I feel safe. I'll still pull from the areas bordering the piece, but the important thing is that I allow the patch of hair *under* the piece to grow. This is where the centre of the whorl lies, the locus of desire.

But by the second week, things loosen: my fingers start to play with the edges of the piece, threading a finger to poke around underneath it, just to feel what has been concealed; where the growth is up to.

And before I know it, my fingers will have worried enough of the edge loose, that I can begin to pull again, from the fresh growth. Just a bit.

It is so tempting to peel back the edges of the hairpiece (like peeling back a bandaid from a scab) and furrow under, just to get to the ones nestled there, which if someone were to witness, would look like I was lifting up my scalp, as though it were some kind of lid over my mind. (And I guess I had fantasised the piece could be a kind of lid, as though my urges could be contained like steam in a simmering pan.) When I'm pulling lately, the piece ends up slipped to one side, barely attached. A bit like one of those fascinator things. My silhouette, when my hair is in this arrangement, looks two-headed.

And then somewhere in the third week: tearing it off. Such a good feeling, to be rid of the thing. Crouched on the floor, it looks like a sleeping pet.

A border of glue remains on my scalp – to dissolve it, I

lather on a cocktail of shampoos and conditioners and soaps, hoping one of them might contain some kind of dissolving ingredient. Then I try to work a comb through my hair, but it snags quickly – big globules of glue lodge themselves into the comb, so I'll try to work them out with another comb, then start tackling my scalp again. Once the hot water runs out all my hair is coated in a waxy kind of residue, and then I will find myself pulling again, the waxiness of the hairs making them grip differently (any slight variation to texture or length represents a new thing for my desire to latch onto). A couple of hours later, another shower. This time as hot as I can, which seems to remove most of the waxy slick. Sometimes, if I'm desperate, I'll put in some turps, but it stings my scalp, with all the freshly opened pores from which I've just extracted hairs. Plus I don't trust myself not to get it in my eyes.

Once the hairpiece has detached itself completely, I will sleep without it. In the mornings, I brush my (actual, biological?) hair: first the curtain of gossamer-thin fringe, and then the back section, try to make it all frizz up a bit, so as to take up as much space as it can. Then I flick the fringe forward to veil my face, position the hairpiece, flick the curtain back over and clip everything into place with three bobby pins – one in the middle, and then one on either side. Then I scoop everything back and tie it into a tight bun. Then a wide headband over the top, to keep everything in place, and to conceal the join where my hair ends and the piece begins, patting around with my fingers to check there's no scalp showing. This all makes me look slightly Amish. It's an ugly hairstyle, but better than the alternative.

This curious cycle also impacts on when I see certain people, how I carry myself around them – at the start, when the piece has been freshly attached, I feel relatively safe. But by the end of the cycle, with my dowdy old headband, I feel newly on the edge of exposure.

It doesn't take long, for me to grow used to the piece, and for my hyper-consciousness to transfer from its presence to its absence, so that the prospect of leaving the house without it comes to feel akin to leaving the house without my shoes.

Each time I return for my appointment, I can't help the feeling of having fallen short, of disappointing Annalise all over again, at all this being futile. But each time she receives my scalp as it is. And I admire her, for her perfect neutrality, her absence of judgement or comment. In her attitude of acceptance, Annalise reminds me of the matter-of-fact, middle-of-the-night way my parents, when I was little, would strip my bed of its sheets when I wet them, tuck me back in with clean, dry ones. Without fuss. (Only as an adult did I learn that my own mother used to wet the bed frequently as a child, and her mother used to drag out the mattress in front of everyone – I don't know whether this was a wilful attempt to shame her, but shame my mother it did.)

I still remember this one time, having lifted off the piece, my head so raw and mortifying, and Annalise, this woman whose job it was to make my hair nice, this woman whose livelihood was hair, saw the tears sliding down my cheeks, and in the mirror our eyes locked and she said, gently, as though she were talking to her own daughter: 'It's okay, it's only *hair*.'

*

I'm thankful that I don't transfer my compulsion to pull out my hair to the piece: it holds zero temptation. I have no interest in its anatomy or its manufacture.

But other things do transfer: the shame, for a start. I'd wished for my shame to disappear, but all that happens is it morphs in form. I come to think of my 'hair' as two distinct parts, conjoined: neither feels complete without the other. The piece looks creepy on its own (in the way of dentures in a glass, or anything bodily that's detached from the body) and my own hair without the piece nestled safely within it looks pitiful. Each is shameful in its own way; and so my shame, instead of softening, gets compounded.

And my fear of exposure transfers, too: from paranoia that people will detect my hair loss, to paranoia that they will detect its fakeness. If I'm riding my bike, crossing countless driveways, and I imagine a car backing out and into me, it is not my injuries that I picture, but the reaction of the paramedics if in the impact my hairpiece flew off.

Another thing that transfers: the sorry state of my scalp to the sorry state of the piece. I have never been good at looking after my things. My bike gets so rusty that every time I take it to the bike shop they tell me it's not roadworthy; I get calls from the library to chide me for returning my books with coffee stains; I once got stopped from checking in to an international flight because my passport was so mouldy.

This isn't some kind of deliberate statement about materialism ... looking after physical possessions has simply never been a priority for me. I have always privileged my internal world over my external one (capturing images in my journal at the end of a day, for example, is far more important to me than vacuuming the carpet) and if I seem to you to have taken this to an extreme, I suspect that is, at some level, tied to my hair-pulling. What I mean is – the appearance of my hair was so upsetting to me that to cope, I tried to deny my embodied self.

I learned, for example, to put my earrings on without a mirror. One night, I was fiddling with my right earring, and was startled when I felt that the ear-hole had expanded, enough that I could press two fingertips together through it. I rushed to the mirror, then, and saw that on account of the fact my ear had become slightly infected and was weeping (had this been for days? weeks? I couldn't say), I'd managed to split my earlobe clean in two. More shocking than the actual split, though, was how long it had taken me to notice. How detached and negligent of my own body – and by extension, of the material world – had I become that I didn't notice a near-one-centimetre split in the most visible part of my ear?

And instead of looking after my piece I let it get knotted, matted even – it is crazy, how quickly hair can felt – and so each time it comes to my appointment I have to face it, lay it out on the carpet and force a comb through it, to tame it. (Sometimes I leave this until the last possible moment, in the train station bathroom, yanking a comb through the piece on my lap.) I think that probably, I can explain the way I treat my hairpiece like this: my refusal to care for it properly is a kind of compensation for all the time my hair has already stolen from me. Or a way to put that time behind me.

I tend to keep things – scourers, tea towels, clothes – long past when other people would probably chuck them out. And so it is with the piece. It gets like steel wool gets after a while, when you've used it too much. Like a pair of scuffed shoes that you keep on wearing; something ageing; something decrepit. When it gets wet, it smells like a wet animal. Like lanolin.

Though it is real hair, it is, of course, dead. Deader than my own hair, which is technically also dead. The piece, obviously, doesn't replenish itself, doesn't grow. It just gets into a sorrier and sorrier state. I try to suppress the thought, but after a good two years of wearing the piece, I know that from the back, the fact I'm wearing some kind of hairpiece is obvious. It has grown near-bald in sections, and sometimes I can't even be bothered to comb them over, so now I have double-decker damage: the upper (fake) layer mimicking the (real) layer underlying it. (When I teach, I plan my lessons so as not to have to face the board too much, because doing so makes me rigid with paranoia.) Plus, my own hair has lost its dye and returned to its mousey brown colour, which is distinct from the rusted brown of the piece, and so either side of the headband is un-matching.

Eventually Annalise starts to prod me: it's nearly time I might start thinking about looking into a replacement ... She must think I'm not cottoning on to all her gentle prodding, and I suspect she has a word to Andrew, who – unusually – comes to see me. He is expert at asking open-ended questions ('Where are we up to with your hair?') but in the mere fact of asking these questions I discern his meaning: *What are you waiting for?* He says he offers all his clients a system where you can borrow money for up to a year interest-free, or else there's also the option of paying things off in monthly instalments (why do people everywhere assume I have no money?) I tell him: 'Actually, I have the money, it's just I don't want to spend it.' He can't hide his bafflement, though, at the fact I persist in walking around with this scraggly object on my head.

Why the resistance to getting a new piece, aside from the obvious expense? Because it would feel like defeat. The first time round felt like defeat enough, but replacement hair for replacement hair? That would make it some kind of ongoing thing: pathetic.

(Eventually – a whole three years after purchasing the original piece – having made no progress with my actual hair, I have no choice but to buy a second piece, and though it, too, now looks so very tired, I cannot bear the thought of buying a third.)

I still haven't quite forgiven Andrew, for that day. The way I saw him look at my hairpiece, the state of it – the obvious disbelief, that I was still using this ... this *thing*.

# RECOVERY

It's surprisingly hard to find good bandaids. Some are so flimsy – as thin and transparent as Glad wrap – it's a struggle to even remove one from its layers of packaging without it sticking to itself. The fabric ones are best, though the edges fray easily, producing a soft little fringe so that, come midday, if I go to write the shadow of my fingers cast upon the page is all feathery-looking. The other thing about the fabric ones is they get grotty very easily, and in the winter you can't really get them wet. If you do, they stay damp.

At the moment, my standard arrangement is to wear four bandaids at a time: one on each of my thumbs and index fingers. Little blindfolds for my pulling. Not enough to stop my compulsions exactly, but at least they interrupt and flatten some of the sensation. My movements are still deft and swift, don't get me wrong, but something feels plugged.

When I leave the house, my impulse is to strip off the two on my right hand, my thinking being this: two bandaged fingers and it's plausible that you burnt yourself, or cut yourself, but two on each hand is surely a bit weird? Suggests something less temporarily wrong?

When I run out of bandaids I use duct tape. M nicked me the one I'm using now from the construction site where he is at the moment (it touched me, that amid the dustiness and swearing and blaring radio he should have thought of me, and my fingers). The one he got is good quality, which doesn't get destroyed with water. The only trouble is that its un-fleshy blueness stands out in public, even when I limit it to two fingers and not four.

In the evenings before bed, I like getting M to tape up my fingers. The intimacy of it. If we're out of bandaids, him asking where the scissors are, finding the tape's end, cutting a length, cutting it in half, and then half again, and sticking it on the back of the chair ready (like I do when wrapping presents) and then crouching opposite me, taking one hand, firmly like a nurse might, positioning the tape and pressing down its ends. At first he'd put it on too tightly, and I'd have to undo it not long after because it was cutting off my circulation. But now he knows the exact tightness required. He knows, too, to carry out this task without turning over my hand, so that my palms stay facing the ceiling, which, I realise, is the same position he holds *his* hands in to pray. (I still don't like my nails to be exposed, not even to him, and without me ever needing to remind him he colludes in this.) Once each tape is wound around he squeezes each fingertip, to ensure the ends are secure as can be. Two nights ago when he did this I winced and he gave me that look, like I'm being precious, or like he can't believe his own strength, and I told him: 'It's not you, it's me – my fingers are tender. I've been using the Opinel to cut away at my fingernails.' (I lay the blade flat, in the same way my father used to do to sharpen my coloured pencils. Whittling away, grip steady so as not to cut into the lead, or in my own case, finger-flesh.)

He freezes then, like I've crossed some kind of line. Like, he was perfectly fine with bandaging me up to stop me from pulling my own hair out – but a knife entering the equation? I try to reassure him: 'The knife is nothing. It's just to stop me from pulling.' If I cut my nails severely enough, any pressure applied to my fingertips (which is necessary to remove a hair) hurts, and this smarting pain is enough to keep me from pulling so much. He breathes out audibly, looks away a second.

It's only in writing this down, that I see how arbitrary these lines are ... the truth is, I could justify just about anything if it meant I stopped pulling. Even slicing at my nails with a kitchen knife enough to draw blood.

'Stop worrying,' I coax.

'Just makes me scared,' he says.

In their unbroken looping of foraging-stroking-pulling-examining-mouthing-swallowing-foraging, my compulsions connect hand, hair, eyes, and mouth in one fluid sweep. I try interrupting this unbroken loop at each of these points of my person, as though each was the site of possible puncture in a deflating tube, and if I managed to seal the right one, I could keep any more air from escaping.

I try not rinsing the conditioner out of my hair, to make it too slick to grip, and when that dries, I douse my hair in olive oil to make it even greasier. I try rubbing Deep Heat into my scalp, hoping my tongue will be scared off by the toxic taste, but instead I grow used to its tip feeling prickly and raw. I try beanies, chewing gum, thimbles (rubber, plastic, metal) – anything to create a physical barrier. I wear a wide cotton headband, wear it so regularly that if I scrunch it up to my nose it has an unwashed smell. A smell that I carry around with me, on top of my goddamn head. A smell of failure.

The internet is replete with lists of tips and tricks to stop pulling: *Buy some paintbrushes, to pick the bristles out of. Play with silly putty to occupy your hands. Decide that hats can be your best friend. Get a pillow you can yank feathers out from. Wear perfume on your hands so that you will realise when your hand is going up to pull out your hair. Lift weights – your arms will be too tired to want to pull. Put glue on your fingers – pulling off dry glue can give you the same satisfactory feeling as when you are pulling.*

Paul (another patient of Penzel's) found that doing homework was a trigger for his pulling. 'I use scotch tape on my fingers so that I will not be able to grab my hair strands. This only works when I'm reading. When I actually have to use my fingers to write, I rub jalapeño peppers on them to avoid the act. Another thing I tried was to punish myself. I would hit the wall very hard with my fist – one time for every strand of hair I would pull.'

In the years before she was diagnosed, Christina Pearson describes her own extreme strategies to limit her pulling: 'I would tape my mouth with wide silver duct tape, pull a ski mask over my head, tie my hands together, sometimes wrapping a rope around my jaw, always internally negotiating, making deals, contracts, threats, constantly fighting, fighting, fighting, to no avail.' Sometimes, at her wits' end, she would drink herself into oblivion, just to give herself some sort of reprieve. (In 1990, Christina founded the Trichotillomania Learning Center, now known as the TLC Foundation for Body-Focused Repetitive Behaviors.)

Thinking about all these efforts to stop, I'm reminded of how skilled our cats became at catching pigeons and mynas and peewees (this was the hierarchy, the pigeons the slowest-witted and slowest-winged), and how we'd put bells on their collars. But they'd perfect that slinky skilful way they learn to stalk, learn which parts of the lawn were best to hide in, and learn to move without dislodging the bell at all. So then we'd attach a second bell, but eventually, they would learn to control these. I'm reminded, too, of those metal spikes you see installed (that I hate), to stop birds from perching or nesting in public places.

None of these interventions curb the impulse: to kill, to nest, to pull. All they do is complicate the process, make the route to the destination more circuitous, up the level of skill or determination or creativity required.

The brain is always one step ahead, always capable of outsmarting whatever devices or barriers or strategies or bandaid solutions are in place.

Here is the basic truth: I wanted to stop pulling, but I also wanted to pull. And one of these desires was always stronger than the other.

*

Discussions of trichotillomania tend to identify two distinct subtypes of pulling: 'focused' and 'automatic' (sometimes labelled 'conscious' and 'unconscious'). Automatic hair-pulling is characterised by pulling without full behavioural awareness, often performed during sedentary situations. Some people might pull their hair while watching TV, for instance, without even realising they're doing it. Or in some cases, while asleep. Focused hair-pulling, on the other hand, is more 'intentional', involving full behavioural awareness and often triggered by intense emotions or unpleasant internal experiences. Most patients report a 'mixed pulling style', depending on the situation and mood.

My own pulling, I think, tends to slip from one mode towards (but never quite into) the other. I always begin with full awareness of my movements, and am utterly convinced, in those initial minutes, that I could stop if I wanted to. This sounds like self-delusion, I know, but sometimes I *do* manage to stop, just to pull one or two hairs, and move on.

(I thought this was an immense achievement, until years after the fact, a psychologist I saw cautioned me, saying that my brain would use the memory of this experience to give me permission forever after to start pulling, like an alcoholic thinking they'd be okay to stop at one drink. Years later, exasperated, when I tried to convey to another psychologist the brute force of my urges, that I had zero power against them, she told me I probably had more power in those moments than I realised. One of them seemed to be saying:

*You have less control than you think*; the other one: *You have more control than you think*. I still can't decide who to believe.)

Soon enough, I can't stop and I find myself caught, swept up in the mechanical urges. And once things escalate, whatever-it-is-that-makes-me-pull can seem as if it were an intelligence outside me. A great wind threatening to carry off those bits of me not properly fastened down. But even then, I don't know that my pulling is wholly 'automatic'. I am entirely aware of what I am doing with my hair, it feels mindful and precise, but I simply am not able to stop. It is both within and outside of my control at once. Is that possible? Who can say to what degree we do *anything* consciously and to what degree our unconscious is at play?

I have never learned to drive, never even got my Ls, but driving is the standard example given to illustrate the phenomenon of automatic functioning. It is optimal, so the theory goes, for our brains to move as many functions as possible to automatic control, since this frees up our attention, and our capacity for higher-level cognitive processing. A beginner driver, so I'm told, will carefully attend to their position within the lane, will purposely activate an indicator before an intersection, whereas for a more experienced driver, most of these behaviours will occur outside their awareness.

Driving on 'automatic pilot' (in the way of experienced drivers) facilitates safe driving, since valuable cognitive processing capacity is shifted away from the mechanical tasks of accelerating, steering, and braking, and freed up for assessing more salient issues, like a potential collision. Freed up, too, for non-driving-related thought (which may explain why some drivers say their best creative thinking happens while driving. Or why some writers will confess to having their best ideas while doing the dishes, or gardening).

I know that when I am *not* pulling, so much of my mind is occupied by the effort of resistance. As is the case for a novice driver, my near-constant calculation and vigilance is exhausting.

Maybe it's fanciful thinking, but I do wonder if the automation of my own pulling is a means of freeing up my mind for thoughts about things-other-than-pulling?

On the lure of her own drinking, Leslie Jamison (in her book *The Recovering*) writes that alcohol 'promised a version of consciousness that didn't mean endless twisting and turning in the bedsheets of myself, tangled and restless'. Even if this was only ever 'a temporary flight'.

The ultimate paradox is this: that it's only when in total surrender to my urges that I feel unburdened of them. Only when I relinquish all control to them, do I feel some respite.

When I'm teaching English, it's far easier to correct mistakes that are newly learned than ones that a student has been making for years, and which they have permanently incorporated into their natural speech (M has been making some of the same so-called mistakes since he first began coming to my classes in Curtin, but I find it hard to bring myself to correct him, even though he asks me to, so embedded a part of him have they become to me). 'Fossilisation' is the technical term for this linguistic process.

The trouble with a task being relegated to automatic functioning is that it can make it very difficult to bring it back into awareness. One theory about what makes a habit like hair-pulling so hard to break relates to this inherent difficulty of unlearning anything.

Methods to reverse hair-pulling behaviours therefore often centre around restoring an individual's awareness. The idea is that only if an individual is *conscious* of their behaviour can they change it. Online, you can find various versions of templates and forms expertly designed to help track one's pulling. These usually require you to document each occasion you pull, and to record information such as your specific location; the time; where on your body you pulled from; the severity of the urges; what happened and how you felt just prior to pulling; and how you felt afterwards. I download the TrichStop app, too, where 'data is conveniently organized and visualized with graphs and charts, which makes gaining insights into your hair-pulling patterns easy'.

In my periodic Google-hunts of you-know-which-word, I've taken to filtering the results to the last month (like someone returning to familiar bushland to check new growth after fire, or rain). In this way I come across Keen: a device that looks like a Fitbit, but that's designed purposely to break habits like nail-biting and hair-pulling. You program it so that it vibrates when your hand goes anywhere near your head/arms (wherever it is that you've set as off-limits), the idea being that this will fast-track your 'journey to awareness', and enable you to 'reclaim your time and energy to go after your dreams!'

When I tell M about my discovery, he makes a face like the one I used to make when a teaching colleague of mine would come in every Monday on some new liquid diet, and each time expect us to be encouraging and excited.

'Adele, aren't you aware enough?' I suspect he's right. Under my bed, I have several dozen notebooks dating back to 2010 (already seven years deep into my illness), each one testing out a new method, each with a newly-refined system of colour-coded stickers, each one devoted to ending this thing once and for all.

Ultimately though, I felt that I'd been appointed detective in a case where I knew, secretly, that I was the guilty party.

The other thing was: no matter how apparently granular the detail captured in these templates, they always ended up striking me as not just reductive, but deceptive.

The days where, according to the record, I didn't pull at all, bothered me especially. I might not technically have removed any hair from my head, but that didn't mean my mind wasn't still utterly consumed by pulling. When I wasn't physically in the act of pulling, I was still anticipating it; trying to suppress this anticipation; figuring out how I could pull; figuring out how I could avoid pulling; berating myself for all the pulling I had already done. Was an ostensibly blank day in my notebook really what progress looked like?

The notebooks appealed to my urge to preserve my experience on the page ... but I suspect that when I didn't have anything concrete to record, I was (subconsciously) compelled to pull, just so the page would better reflect my internal obsession.

At times, I thought it important to understand the times and the places when I *didn't* pull. But then wasn't I effectively recording *everything*, analysing my entire existence through the one lens?

The profound unfairness at the heart of this affliction-of-mine is that each individual hair takes but a fraction of a second to be removed, but so very long a time to return. Perhaps this is why, driven to undo months of growth in a split second, I often feel I have retreated in time. Perhaps this is why I keep needing to return to that space, where time dissolves.

Underneath all my obsessive monitoring, the truth was that entering that expansive space, that I could only enter through pulling, was still the feeling I was most interested in having.

That space was always there, ready to be tapped. Like the ocean-sound in shells that lies waiting, ready to be pressed to the ear.

'Though you might repeat the experience millions of times in 30 or 40 or 50 years, the prime thrill never fades. It looks repetitive but no ride is ever the same; it feels like a miracle every time you do it and I'd hate to lose that sense of wonder.'

Those are not my words, but Tim Winton's. He is not writing about pulling, but about surfing (which I've never had any inclination to attempt), and yet the sentiment resonates so strongly with me: the perennial thrill of it; the surrender and submission; the way its miracle can only be fathomed from inside, and not from without ... 'To surf, a person foregoes timetables and submits to the vagaries of nature ... The child of a pragmatic, philistine and insular culture, I responded to the prospect of something wilder, broader, softer, more fluid and emotional'.

The most powerful accounts of the lure and the glory of my disease I've chanced upon when not looking. I have collected hundreds of examples of these, copying them out by hand. Perhaps this is just my own obsession: my illness so totalising that I see its shadows everywhere. But it is also, I think, proof of more universal hungers: to leave behind wherever we are; to have a secret space we can call our own; to reach for the sublime.

By now, I'm fully aware that – statistically speaking – I am most likely to pull between two and three in the afternoon, when my energy naturally dips; after an argument; just before having a shower; if I don't eat at the right time and end up hangry; at my computer if I don't take sufficient breaks; in the library bathroom. I am unlikely to pull: at my F45 class; while in conversation; eating; swimming. No matter how meticulously I trace the patterns of my pulling, though, just beneath the surface of the scalp lies another, hidden pattern, that I have never seen any app or template allude to or attempt to capture.

The thing that can't be reliably predicted (only ever intuited) is whether a hair you zoom in on has a root attached or not. Pull five hairs, for example, and the ratio of rootless to root-attached hairs (and the particular sequence in which they emerge) will be as unpredictable as a hand of playing cards. *This* pattern is never the same.

Hair-pulling has been likened to barbering in animals; it also puts me in mind of Skinner's famous rats. B.F. Skinner discovered that rats pressed a lever for food more steadily when they did not know when the next food pellet was coming than when they *always* received the pellet after pressing. And similarly in the case of people like me: if every hair had a root attached (or even every third hair), then the process wouldn't be nearly as compelling.

If say I pull five hairs and *none* of them have roots attached, then I am driven to keep going (because my chances, I figure – however illogically – should now be maximised, and the root when it does arrive will feel more hard-earned). Pull *with* some roots, and I'm driven to keep going (because roots tend to congregate in the one patch of head). In other words, it makes no difference what I have just pulled: it's the inconsistency and unpredictability of what is still to come that makes pulling so irresistible.

In psychology, this is known as 'intermittent reinforcement', and is considered the most powerful formula to get someone to feel or act in a desired way; a method that has been determined to yield the greatest effort from the subject. It is what makes poker machines so highly addictive. It is also, disturbingly, a hallmark method used by abusers, who will use periodic affection or small acts of kindness to their advantage, which are said to keep the victim bonded to their abuser.

*

My mind has become expert at justifying each single pull.

Before I've commenced pulling on any given day (the parameters of a day feel significant: once pulling has been set in motion then for the remainder of that day, not-pulling becomes as painstaking as trying not to blink and I need to wait for the next day, for a clean slate), in that precise moment when I have a single hair ready, holding it with just that exact amount of tension that means I am on the precipice of removing it or letting it be, this is what happens in my mind:

If overall, my hair is growing back and getting a bit of thickness to it, then I think: *Okay, you can pull a bit now because there's enough growth for any damage not to matter too much*. But if my scalp is stubbly and patchy: *Well, it's already in a sorry state, so whether you pull or not, it's going to stay looking awful for months. So you may as well.*

Plus: *If you don't pull at all, that doesn't really require that much effort now, does it. Pull a bit and set things in motion, and then stop – that'll be more impressive, that'll mean you're making progress.*

When I convince myself that pulling *this one hair* won't actually make any difference in the scheme of things, what makes my resistance near-impossible is that this thought is, essentially, *true*. Multiply that singular truth a thousand times over, and its truth collapses, but in the mindscape of this disease, it's impossible to think that far ahead of *this* hair, just *this* one, *here*.

I convince myself not to use all the many things I know will help. Partly this is the addict in me, hungry to pull at all costs. Partly it is because I still see taped-up fingers and slippery hair as cheating. I want to learn the truth about my situation. In the same way, I never take painkillers for period pain: I want to know what is there, bare and unvarnished, however painful that may be, and however illogical that may sound.

I rip off the bandaids, and then if I can stave off the pulling, there's a small thrill to it, like riding a bike for the first time without training wheels. This progress feels more *real*.

Sometimes, my options are not 'pull vs don't pull', but rather 'pull now vs pull later'. My logic (if it warrants that word) goes like this: this hair is *not* going to last where it is; even if I'm able to summon up resistance this time and the next and the next, best-case scenario I can keep it a week, so I may as well pull it out now so as not to give myself false hope about having saved it. If I get rid of it now, then I can rid myself of that constant hum of desire surrounding it. And plus then it can begin growing again! If I pull it out *now* as opposed to in a week's time, then in one month's time I'll be one full week ahead.

An alcoholic will measure their progress in days of sobriety, and a relapse will mean setting the tally back to zero. I try adopting this framework for myself: go a day without pulling, add one to the tally; pull at all, and be forced to begin over again. But my capacity to justify pulling at whatever cost worms its way into this space, too.

In that tiny window of time after I have pulled just one hair: *I'll count this as a slip; I ought to cut myself some slack. A little mistake isn't the end of the world, I can still record this as an overall successful day.*

Then I pull just a couple more: *These are only slips. I'm only human after all!*

And once I've crossed the point where I know in my heart I am obliged to return the count to zero, well, then it feels wasteful *not* to pull more. The day is going to be marked as a failure, regardless of what happens from this point on (the same feeling as having paid a certain amount for a buffet dinner, and then only having picked at some of the salad – must keep going back for more, to get my money's worth).

I usually picture my brain as slimy sausage-like ropes, coiled up in my skull. But all this rationalising and justifying feels like it belongs in its own compartment: a well-oiled device implanted somewhere in there, that whirrs into motion at the slightest touch.

Finding a reason to pull no matter what has become my modus operandi. All grooves of thought, however labyrinthine or however implausible, all lead back to the one place: the place that says, *pull*.

And yet, I am forever fantasising about allowing my hair to grow back. Periodically, I google the speed at which hair grows: 1.5 centimetres a month. Then I click through to page two of the search results to check there's not some other opinion on the matter – but no, this seems to be the consensus. I am always brewing new plans in my head, mentally removing tape measures of time. *If I stop now, then in six months that'll give me nine centimetres*. I try to make use of each new month, each turn of the year, to give me some new resolve. Is that crazy? To rely on something as arbitrary as a line in time to propel you?

Once I reach a few days pull-free in a row, there is more reason to keep not-pulling, to see the number tick up and up. I find it gets easier and easier with each day, like I'm gaining momentum, and I start to believe that maybe finally, *finally* this thing is behind me, has run its course. But the higher the number gets, the more charged the whole process becomes. Like a jackpot. To be able to undo so much work and so much resistance in one swift flick of the fingers is its own weird kind of power.

It's tempting to see trichotillomania as a total failure of willpower; a total relinquishing to base urges and impulses that others are powerful enough to resist.

But what an outsider can't realise about this affliction is the *immense* amount of willpower involved. For any one of my hairs to reach a certain length requires inordinate patience, and a thousand small acts of resistance. If it weren't for willpower then I would be utterly at the mercy of my urges; I wouldn't be functional in the ways I continue to be.

Last night, and the night before that, too, and the one before that, come to think of it (this seems to be a new pattern forming), I felt that I *was* acutely alert while pulling, but that my hands were being controlled by some separate system. It wasn't that I was fighting to control myself, or my mind, or even my fingers, but just completely separate from any of them. Like if it's pouring rain and you're stuck under an eave without an umbrella, and you're waiting for it to ease so you can make a dash for the next shelter; that kind of weak wishing was all the power I was capable of exerting. Something unbelievable about it, having all will wrested from you like that. Despite these recurrent plunges into near-paralysis, even I myself fall into the trap, still, of believing that if I am ever to truly stop, then I will need to summon all my *will* to do so.

I used to think of anorexia as trichotillomania's inverse when it came to the question of will. Starvation as iron will made manifest; hair-pulling as total abandon. It therefore confounded me, reading Fiona Wright's *Small Acts of Disappearance*, how bodily my shock of recognition felt.

Both are attempts at control. Both involve utter loss of control: the hair-puller doesn't want to pull, but can't help it; the anorexic doesn't want to starve herself, but can't help it. (I do hate the connotations of the word 'control'– it summons to me someone with colour-coordinated accessories and Post-it notes, whereas when I use that word 'control' what I mean is: not disappearing into the abyss.)

I remember hearing Wright say in an interview that an anorexic friend of hers had come up with an analogy to explain to non-anorectics the excruciating difficulty of eating: she said it was as if you were presented with a shoe on a plate, and instructed to eat it. I love this image, the way it captures how extreme and ridiculous something so apparently basic (ingesting food or, in my case, not tearing out your own hair) can come to be.

Both conditions restructure and eventually consume the mind, and involve endless calculation and vigilance, creating their own sealed worlds. Both make visible inner feelings of aberrance or wrongness; both steep the individual in shame. And the state of hunger (which Wright describes as 'an attempt to transcend the body, to become something more') reminds me of the fugue-like state of pulling, in which time thickens and distends. Both are their own forms of subtraction, at making the body take up less space.

So clear now are all these parallels I don't know why it took me so long to see them. I suspect it is society that muddied my thinking. Our society's feminine ideal is thin, with flowing tresses. Anorexia appears to approach this ideal (and to take it to an extreme), whereas trichotillomania departs from it.

That anorexia is wilful is erroneous thinking. And so, too, is the notion that a hair-puller can cure themselves through sheer force of will. But I struggle, still, to accept this. I still feel that I ought to be trying harder, that I should be dealing with this better than I am.

Last week, I came home after lunch near-euphoric at having written something half-good, uncharacteristically optimistic in myself. But after a nap, vicious thoughts arrived: *You're pathetic, as if you'll ever be a writer, your writing is still so goddamn amateur*. When I relayed this to M on the balcony that evening —his tea in a mug, drunk seconds after being boiled, sugar cubes rattling in his mouth; me waiting for mine to cool — without hesitation, he said: 'But don't you see?'

'See what?'

'That's just another thought to make you pull.'

Perhaps you will see all my failures to stop as self-sabotage.

I see them as something more elemental, something that gets to the very core of who I am.

It is true, that living so long in this sick body, I feel estranged from the person I once was, and from the person I might otherwise have been, and there is grief in this. But because I have pulled my entire adult life, when I *don't* pull, I also feel estranged, and there is a curious grief in this, too. Always a feeling that I am not quite ready to say goodbye to she who pulls. I will, but just not yet.

I know I told you earlier that I longed to restore my hair to its original state, to how I am *meant* to look. But in those stretches of time when my hair has managed to begin to replenish itself and return to its 'natural' state, I have a feeling that this non-pulling body isn't mine either – that it's inauthentic and trying to pose as someone it's not.

When I stave off pulling, part of me feels I am denying the power of the act. Like I'm being insolent; overstepping; tempting fate. I ought to have some humility in the face of this thing.

Is this my illness talking? It's hard to know anymore.

I still don't know what recovery looks like, nor even how I might measure such a thing. I know that I am not 'better'. I still pull. I don't pull as much as I once did, but I still pull a lot, by any measure. My life hasn't got any easier; maybe I've just ceased to be surprised at how difficult this life can be.

I used to think a disease like this would have an arc, like a story does, with a climax, would run its course and reach its natural logical conclusion.

'When I returned to myself each morning,' writes Jamison, 'the groove of lack had just grown deeper, more stubbornly etched – like a skip, skip, skip in the song.'

Now, I wonder whether I was in fact closer to a conclusion at the start of my illness, when the pathological grooves of my mind were not so deep. I have always, since the start, been trying to recover – if trying to recover means trying to stop, or trying to return to the state that was. I am terrified that the longer I keep on pulling, the further I am from any possibility of what we call 'recovery'.

I regard my life as cleaved in two: the child, who hadn't yet discovered pulling, and the adult, who had.

And I still can't help but see the world as cleaved in two: those who pull, and those who don't. (A member of the former I am yet to meet. Once, M spotted a young woman on a train, doing the thing I do. He passed her his number: 'My girlfriend has the same problem as you,' he whispered. Another time, someone I follow on Twitter tweeted about her sister tearing out her hair; I tried my best to track the sister down, but to no avail.) My fundamental orientation to those not of my kind still revolves around my fear of exposure. I don't think I ever believed in a magic bullet, but I thought that if I *tried* hard enough, that would allow me to cross over, to leave my kind behind. And then, a spectacular change would come over me.

But increasingly, to picture myself as a person who doesn't pull feels as distant and as implausible as returning to my girlhood.

More and more, I think of recovery as a myth, and

adulthood, too: perhaps there are no lines to be crossed; there are no magical transformations from one state into another. Maybe whatever has come before gets enfolded and contained within us, in the way of rings in a tree, so that if you were to slice through my future self, who I still sometimes imagine – she who has long, dark-and-shot-with-silver curls – inside you would find my girl-self, and also the self who was yet to find a way to live her life that meant she did not need to escape into temporary flight.

# PSYCHOLOGISTS

In those brief interludes of this century during which I felt released from the spell of my compulsions, I came to scorn those who pulled their hair. I saw them as pathetic and weak-willed: how could they not quit their embarrassing and awful habits? Like someone newly escaped from a cult, I was incredulous and mortified that I had been a follower for so long; that I had been brainwashed by a mode of thinking and operating that was so patently concocted.

And then, again, I would slip. My belief would be renewed, my faith restored.

It is astounding to me, now, to think that from the onset of my illness in 2003, it took me precisely one decade to even contemplate seeking professional help. It seemed so important to me, through all those years, that I solve this thing for myself, as though it were a riddle, or a test of strength, and as though asking someone for help was a form of cheating.

I lurched between two seemingly contradictory fears. First, that this problem of mine was too small to be taken seriously: out in the world there were children without food, people without roofs over their heads ... I couldn't shake the nagging belief that my troubles were of my own making, and therefore not actually *real*. I didn't know of anyone in my admittedly limited social circles who had ever seen a psychologist (it seems to me that in the years since 2013, when I secretly sought out therapy, people's openness around these matters has grown dramatically). At the time, there seemed something self-indulgent and melodramatic about the very prospect.

My second fear: that this problem of mine was larger than could be believed. It sounded implausible, if not downright ridiculous. How had such a trivial gesture come to monopolise my existence? How could something so small take up so much space? Writer Karl Ove Knausgård says that because he was an 'artist', he could 'cut off his own ear ... spew out obscenities ... maybe even shoot up some heroin in his bathroom'. Oh, how deeply shameful he finds it, then, that the thing he ends up addicted to is *chewing gum*. Like him, I found myself wishing that I had a proper problem to present. A different, more magnificent failing.

I imagined therapy would offer generic solutions and platitudinous advice. It would turn me into a cookie-cutter person, and what I thought of as my true self (my secret, pulling self) would be destroyed. My suffering might be eased, but there would be something falsifying about the process. I was, unknowingly, subscribing to the myth that Susan Sontag sought to dismantle: that if you were ill you were 'more conscious, more complex psychologically'; that psychological turmoil was 'proof of inner depths'.

In the end, it wasn't determination or epiphany that led me to seek help – just sheer exhaustion. The harder I tried to stop, the more my pulling spiralled out of control, and I'd got to the point where my compulsions were consuming in excess of six or seven hours of my every day. I'd reached my limit. All my energy and all my willpower was spent. Seated before my very first psychologist to confess the nature of my problem (that was how I saw it: as confession; my absolution in his hands) I was quivery and fragile and desperate. He grinned stupidly, rubbed his hand over his bald pate, and said: 'I can sympathise.'

We embarked upon a series of sessions of EMDR – Eye Movement Desensitisation and Reprocessing – an approach that involves the patient recalling distressing images while holding a small, pulsating electrode in each hand, simultaneously keeping track of a stimulus (in my case, the therapist's hand) that alternates from one side to the other. Originally developed to treat PTSD in soldiers, the theory is that the patient's rapid eye movements dampen the power of emotionally charged memories of past traumatic events. (Alongside Trauma-Focused CBT, EMDR is recognised as the treatment of choice for PTSD by the American Psychiatric Association, the World Health Organization and the US Department of Defence). This was not a treatment I sought out – this therapist just happened to be attached to the bulk-billed inner-suburban medical centre where my GP practised, and this approach just happened to be the one to which he subscribed. He said nobody understood why this method worked, but that it did, and that he'd never treated anyone with my particular problem, but that it was worth a go. And it couldn't do any harm ...

When I expressed my skepticism at this pseudo-science to M, he told me it was important to trust the therapist, otherwise the therapy might not work. (This was the first year of our relationship; the first year of M's release from detention.) I needed so badly to believe in my capacity to be fixed – that was how I conceived of myself at that time, like an engine with a fault – that I suppressed my doubts, and I'd had plenty of practice in suppression by that point. I might find it hard to take the therapist's bizarre methods seriously, but surely he must struggle to believe in the power or logic of my perverse afflictions? My mind was so warped, so crazed, that who knew what strange treatment I would need to undergo?

Ultimately, though, for all the faith I managed to summon, EMDR did nothing to alleviate my compulsions. The extent of his advice for me then was this: that I should try sitting on my hands, and see what happened.

The next psychologist I was referred to, in 2014, knew the name of my condition, and had treated other people with it. And he didn't make any flippant comments (I'll admit, it was a low bar I was working with here).

Where the mechanisms of EMDR struck me as vaguely New-Agey, this man dealt in hard data, using the methods of CBT. I slipped into the role of scientist, conducting experiments on myself, reporting the results back to him for his analysis. Over several months, I kept meticulous records of my pulling habits, so as to identify the patterns of where and at what time and how frequently I pulled, and to identify my 'triggers'. At one stage he had me collect the hairs I pulled each day, place them in individual, dated envelopes, and store them together in a drawer. At another stage, as a disincentive (he didn't use the word 'punishment') to pulling, I was to send him a text each time I pulled. This was supposed to interrupt the circuit of pulling. And when I was entering a situation where I knew I was likely to pull (e.g. having a shower) I was first to visualise the entire process (turning the doorknob, removing my top, etc.) so as to heighten my consciousness of my fingers, my thoughts, and try to unpick and unlearn what had become an entirely automatic process. I also remember having to sit at scheduled times facing my bedroom mirror, and practise going through the motions of pulling, but resisting *actually* pulling, and this exercise was supposed to desensitise me.

My compulsions, I sometimes thought, were a bit like the cockroaches that used to plague my share-house (we had ones of all sizes, the occasional albino one, too, and at one stage we would have to fish the baby ones out of our tea). They say for every insect visible, there are at least a hundred more hidden. We kept trying new kinds of traps and poisons, hoping that over time their population would diminish, and eventually die out. But they were invincible, the creatures and the compulsions both.

This therapist's methods were seductive in how methodical, measurable, and systematic they appeared to be. In her exploration of her own skin-picking disorder, Eleanor Limburg writes that there is indeed something very appealing about the sort of explanation that sees the sufferer as stuck in a behavioural loop. Viewed from this perspective, 'it is not "I" who picks but "it". There is no meaning to "its" behaviour: it is like a pianola following the notes on a punchcard, just because that is what it does'. And most seductively of all, an explanation like this, 'lets you off that exhausting quest for meaning'.

The other appealing thing about it is that it made me believe that once I landed on the right solution I would be returned to my original, un-sick self. As if my pulling was an abscess that could be excised. Esmé Weijun Wang, in her memoir *The Collected Schizophrenias*, admits how comforting it can be to think of mental illness as a transparency overlaid on an 'unblemished self'; 'that there is, deep down, an impeccable self without disorder'. But at what point does such a belief become delusion? Wang concludes: 'there may be no impeccable self to reach, and if I continue to struggle towards one, I might go mad in the pursuit'.

I had always been the model student, and now I became the model patient. Diligent, trusting, and disciplined. I followed his instructions to the letter; I suggested improvements and refinements to the templates he gave me; I did my homework religiously; I did not challenge his authority. Incrementally, my pulling subsided, and I lapped up his praise.

For several surreal months I thought I had been cured. I can't say, now, what it was that lured me to return to my ways. But return I did, and though I berated myself for it, it also felt like a homecoming. My urges hadn't been destroyed at all, only made dormant; and now they were like creatures scuttling out of hibernation.

Where the cognitive-behavioural strategies focused squarely on my hair-pulling to the exclusion of all else, my next psychologist (randomly assigned by a random GP, but with whom I have stayed from 2015 to this day) never seemed all that fussed about the specifics of my compulsions. Her own belief, she once told me, is that while CBT may be effective in the short term, it is fairly superficial, and doesn't get to the heart of the problem. In her analysis, my previous psychologist had 'colluded' with me, offering a 'grab-bag' of strategies but not ever exploring *why* it was I pulled in the first place. My hair-pulling, so her refrain goes, is 'just a symptom'.

To her mind, it is the stuff underneath that matters: whether a patient starves themselves, cuts themselves, drinks too much, or gambles, or pulls out their hair, is arbitrary.

Even so, it was she who once asked me why it was I'd been drawn to pull my hair, rather than some other vice ... I don't think she meant that I'd selected it, exactly, but rather that my being drawn to this particular affliction over others was not entirely random.

It is strange, to think of all the different possible afflictions, each existing with their own intact form, and that through God knows whichever confluence of genes and circumstances and fate, a person is more likely to acquire one habit over another.

And it is true, I see now, that part of the allure of pulling must have been the fact that it is a solitary activity conducted away from others' eyes, in the way that smoking weed or drinking beer typically isn't. I have never liked activities that require too much equipment or financial outlay or involve too much negotiation with other people. In not being reliant on anyone else, pulling out my own hair was in perfect accord with the self-sufficiency I have always striven for.

Chris Fleming, reflecting on the origins of his own drug-taking, writes that as far back as he can remember, he has envisaged himself as 'permeable, porous', his body 'open to the unpredictable forces of outside matter'. He has always seen himself in terms of what he'd 'swallowed or been immersed in'. When I read that, I thought: *I am the precise opposite*. I have always seen myself as contained, guarded, and impenetrable, and had a fear of foreign bodies entering my own (until well into my twenties I was unable to even swallow a Panadol).

In the years prior to anorexia's 'popularization', writes Hilde Bruch, anorexia was the 'accomplishment of an isolated girl who felt she had found her own way to salvation'; each considered herself the 'original inventor of this misguided road to independence'. (Bruch's use of the word 'popularization' is odd: media attention and medical interest in anorexia may have increased anorexia's visibility, but the condition has existed for a long time, tied to religiosity in the mediaeval period, and classified as a medical disorder in 1874.)

By the seventies, says Bruch, the disease had shifted from being a 'solitary experience' to a 'shared generational phenomenon'. Louise Glück writes that she had never heard of anorexia when she became sick in the late fifties ... if she had, she suspects she'd have felt 'so stymied ... to have a disease so common, so typical' that she would have been obliged to 'devise some entirely different gestures to prove my uniqueness'. (In fact, Glück's insistence on her own singularity remains an incredibly common sentiment among anorexics, even today.)

In retrospect, I see that this was another part of hair-pulling's allure: the fact that for so long, I didn't know that it was a *thing*. My teenage self – like Glück, like so many other lonely girls – was repelled by anything conformist or cliched. I would have baulked at the idea of my perfect secret invention fitting a template. In other words, my not-knowing that my illness existed was a precondition for coming to know it as intimately as I have.

My psychologist can't be much over forty. She has neatly groomed blond hair, red lipstick, clear skin, the good toned legs of a runner. She doesn't strike me as the op-shopping type; her wardrobe seems to get updated with each season.

In one of my twenty Medicare-funded sessions of 2020 (double the usual number, thanks to coronavirus) she asks if I can show her my hair, what it looks like when it's out. I wince, and she leans forward, sharply – rare for her – and wants to know how her request makes me feel.

'It's just ... intrusive. And like, I don't see the point.'

'How do you imagine someone reacting if they saw?'

'Disgusted. Obviously. And ... even if they didn't betray any disgust I'd know that they were just concealing it. They'd think: *What has she done to herself? How can she do that? Why doesn't she stop?*'

'And if someone *was* disgusted, you don't think you could handle that?'

'No, because it would be confirmation for me, that I am disgusting; that if people saw the truth about me they would find me disgusting. Plus I just don't think I could possibly deal with someone else's disgust on top of my own.'

'I thought that maybe if you could show me, then maybe we could use it as a springboard for discussion.'

'I just don't know why I'd subject myself to that. It would feel masochistic.'

'Personally, I don't think I'd find the sight of your scalp disgusting. I suspect I'd more likely see someone ... someone in a lot of pain.'

I don't permit her the opportunity to find out.

The conviction I have – that the uninitiated would find my habits revolting – aligns to the view I have long held of myself as unfeminine and unclean. This is another way in which this affliction feels tailor-made for me. But along with trichotillomania's inherent ugliness, there is a secret intricate beauty and order to it, too, and I know I am drawn to this.

My mother likes to tell the story of how once, when I was very little, we were in a library and she put me down so

I could play with the toys while she looked around. When she returned she saw I'd arranged all the toys into little piles according to colour and size, and that was the moment she realised – I forget how she put it exactly – that I was *special.* She recounts this, I know, as illustration of my precociousness. But does it contain something else? Some seed of my need to make patterns, to attach meaning, and, even as a child, an inability to just sit and play?

Papa chimed in once, when she told it: *You're always arranging things into patterns.* He was right. When he eats a mandarin, he stuffs several segments into his mouth at once, seeds and all. Whereas I have always held each individual segment up to the light, like a jewel, to see the silhouette of seeds, and then I carefully peel away all of the membrane. (As a girl, I'd even want to see inside the seeds themselves – these have their own individual casing, and if you carefully strip this off with your teeth, inside are two perfect halves, waxy smooth and immaculate.) And after finishing a mandarin, I tear the peel into small pieces, arranging it on my plate into a design so artful and fastidious that it's always seemed a shame to sweep it into the compost.

I don't know, now, whether years of therapy have led me to see such precursors everywhere ... whether my illness is colouring my entire past, stretching all the way back to infancy? 'The present rearranges the past,' writes Rebecca Solnit. 'We never tell the story whole because a life isn't a story; it's a whole Milky Way of events and we are forever picking out constellations from it to fit who and where we are.'

*

Thanks to Google, in 2020 I come across one Dr Vladimir Miletic, a Russian psychologist with a special interest in trichotillomania. He has created a series of 'webinars' on the subject (which I predictably binge) that reveal his obvious fascination with the subject, his sense that it is worthy of serious analysis and dissection. He is nerdy, self-deprecating, in the habit of illustrating concepts with Modernist artworks, and I take an immediate liking to him.

In Miletic's framing, a repetitive physical act (like hair-pulling or skin-picking or nail-biting) reflects an underlying mental activity. While it's not intuitive to think of trichotillomania as 'useful', Miletic says that every habit is established for a reason; every habit *does* something. Leslie Jamison echoes this sentiment when she reflects that alcohol addiction 'did something a little different for each person I met'. It could represent 'a source of comfort; a means of escaping from intolerable situations; a language, if a garbled one, in which to express our anger and unhappiness'. I found it helpful to reframe my pulling in this way: to see it as an attempted (albeit ineffective) solution to a real problem.

It feels naive now to write this, but the truth is that in all the pre-2013, pre-therapy years I spent pulling, I never really stopped to think about the purpose of my disease – it was something visited upon me; a curse. It was very easy to go from: *I can't see any obvious explanation for why I pull* (and medicine can't decide on one, and doesn't appear to be that invested in finding one) to: *There probably is none*. But for

Miletic, a habit that is deeply entrenched most likely has a density of meaning – so much meaning, in fact, that it can be hard to see.

Miletic draws heavily on the work of psychologist George Kelly, who posited that our psychological life takes place on different levels of cognitive awareness. Some parts of our experience can be easily expressed with words, others not – sometimes we might find art or sound can better express them. And the deeper down into our cognition we go, the more our body comes into play: *this* is where habits abide.

As someone with a deeply ingrained conviction that my habits were infantile and repulsive, it was no easy feat for me to approach my compulsions in this way. I had long privileged my mind over my body (and in a culture like mine, which seems to believe the one can be split off from the other, perhaps this is unsurprising). My mind had endless potential whereas my body betrayed me, regularly reverted to the compulsions of an animal. How could the strange rituals that played out on my scalp possibly reveal anything about the mind? It seemed topsy-turvy. Miletic tells us that a habit like hair-pulling 'is its own kind of language ... contains its own messages'.

So what did my disease know about me that I didn't?

Ever since I was a child, I have felt things too strongly. When we went fishing, I couldn't bear to thread a length of worm onto my hook, and would have to ask someone else to do it for me; I would keep scungy old bandaids on my knees and elbows for too long because I couldn't bear the pain of them being ripped off, and when my strung-out mother would rip them off when I had my back turned, I would feel a deep sense of betrayal.

I was most sensitive of all towards my mother. Even if I was not in the same room, I was hyper-aware of her mood. My mother was a good mother; *is* a good mother. And so I find it hard to know how to convey to you how frightening I found her, what it is about her that I so feared. Instead I want to tell you about an evening from my childhood (I must have been going on thirteen) because I find it easier to talk about these things obliquely.

It must have been a Monday, because that was when I had my piano lesson, and this particular Monday evening my mother had prepared butternut pumpkin soup. Our salt shaker was old; its holes were clogged and its metal thread all salt-encrusted. We were always to taste our food before adding any salt (our mother scorned those who sprinkled salt before tasting), and I did, and decided it needed a little more, but as I was shaking the top came right off and an enormous amount of salt ended up in the soup. I mixed it in, and ate as much as I could bear, between huge gulpfuls of water (waste was forbidden: my mother's refrain when I did not appreciate something: 'Do you know how *hard* Papa has to work to pay for that?'). Unable to finish it, I slid my bowl along to Papa, who always ate all our leftovers (in the same way he used the bathwater after we three had). Somehow, without betraying it to Mama, he made a face to me to convey how revolting it tasted, and then he, silently, force-fed himself as much as he could while I went hungry.

What does this scene reveal about our fear of her, and of her reprimands: that we would sooner eat something inedible and uncomplainingly, in silence, than admit to a simple mistake? Seated around that table (which was round, because my mother didn't like tables with angles) I recall now how important it was for us to always keep the peace; how ill-equipped we were for even the most basic of communication; how we needed to keep my mother calm at all costs. That the smallest of demands or protests felt like a risk not worth taking.

Why, you may be wondering, should I remember such an uneventful evening so vividly? Because earlier that day I had seen my father cry, and so rarely have I seen this that each of the occasions has stayed with me. These were the years when my parents made their living picking fruit.

My mother was always chiding my father – bookish to an extreme – for busting his guts working such long hours for so little pay, and not finding a job where he could use his brain.

And so he had begun to do some translating work. This particular day he had got a train into the city, where he'd managed to get a short contract doing simultaneous interpreting. It was a big deal. He didn't own a suit, so as a family we had all gone on a special trip to Lowes to buy one. How strangely dignified it made him.

That evening, he walked up the driveway. Usually when he came home, no matter how tired he was, he would play with us in the backyard, but this evening was different. His eyes were wet. He called me over, told me through tears that he couldn't do the job, it was too difficult – he just, he couldn't keep up. And then he told me: 'Go and tell Mama, ma grande.' I understood perfectly: he couldn't face her himself. I knew shame intimately; I had faced her judgement, and I did my best never to have to experience it again.

And so I, the dutiful messenger, translated the fact of his tears to my mother. As a child, I don't know that I understood the nature of what must have been his humiliation – I do remember thinking: *Oh no, so much money for a suit that will never again be worn*. I remember taking my father's side when for days afterward my mother would scoff at his 'nervous breakdown'.

Looking back on that evening now, I see the larger, more enduring truths it reveals about my family. That vulnerability was off-limits. That there was something about my mother that felt threatening and unsafe, even to a grown man. That my parents were incapable of difficult adult conversation. As a family we rarely felt like one unit; there was always an ongoing shifting of alliances: my sister and I leaping to my father's defence; my mother and I siding against my sister; my mother and sister against me. There was a tenderness in my father he tried never to expose. And in the face of one another's hurt or sadness, nobody seemed to know how to comfort, or console.

At the start of one our sessions, just as I'm sitting myself down (paranoid, always, at this time of the month, that I am going to bleed onto her pale-grey-linen couch), my psychologist puts her fingers in her mouth. I try to tell myself it's nothing, but then she starts *chewing* at her nail, says hello to me with fingers still in her mouth. Which throws me – how dare she imitate me, just to see how I react.

'Why are you doing that?'

'What?'

'With your fingers.'

'Sorry, I was just getting some orange out of my teeth.'

'You weren't ... you weren't imitating me?'

'No, no I wasn't. But I'm curious to know why you might think that?'

'It's just I've read about it somewhere, part of a treatment plan thing for hair-pulling, where the therapist mirrors the client's body language ...'

'Gosh, no. I assure you it wasn't anything designed to manipulate you, or test you in any way. Just before you arrived, I had an orange, and some got stuck between my teeth.'

I feel ridiculous – so wounded by someone picking orange from her teeth!

'This does raise the question of trust, though ... your difficulty in trusting another, at feeling safe in their presence.'

She admits that she herself was a bit self-conscious around me, because of her own nails – they looked 'disgusting', the polish starting to chip.

I pull her up on the word that she doesn't let me use about my own hands.

'Well, I guess I just meant it's not a very professional look, is it. That's all.'

'But you did use the word "disgusting". And whenever someone does that, uses that word about their nails or their hair, then it makes me feel twice as disgusting.'

'Help me understand?'

'Well, because the reality is your nails look perfectly fine. And then I think: God, if she saw the state of my hands, then imagine how she'd react.'

'It's interesting that that's the place your mind goes to, rather than seeing it as an alignment.'

'But it's not an "alignment". You can't put the two in the same basket.'

'Why not?'

'Because my nails are extreme. I always have to take everything to an extreme. Someone else, if they say they bite their nails they mean they might chew them a bit occasionally, whereas I do it totally compulsively – I use a knife.'

At this, her ears prick up: 'I don't think we've shared around that before?'

'Well, my teeth can only get so far ... Now my nails are too short for teeth to be able to do much, but with the knife, if I hold it flat, I can get them further down.'

It is only very recently that I have been able to understand that when you are upset, it is quite natural to seek out someone for comfort. I had, ever since I was a child, comforted myself and I have always wanted to be self-reliant (a pattern, which, according to my therapist, has resulted in what she calls my 'self-soothing behaviours': nail-biting, hair-pulling). Not needing anyone was a kind of power.

Around my mother, I was hyper-conscious. I measured the rare words I did speak for fear of using the wrong one, and often found silence safest. On the occasions I did need something of her – permission to meet friends at Penrith Plaza, say – I would wait, sometimes for several days, until I could catch her in a pocket of calm. (Even now, writing these lines, some vestigial fear rises in me, and my left thumb traces each of its neighbouring nails along their serrated edges.)

'What is it you'd want to say to her now, if you could?'

I fumble: 'Whatever I said, I know it would hurt her.'

'But if you could, what would you tell her?'

'I don't know, I'd be so scared to choose the wrong words. And then I'd be plagued by guilt, and regret, so what would be the point?'

'But she's not here. She's not in the room with us. You can say anything you like.'

'Probably that: I wish she realised how scared I was of her. I wish she understood how extreme her behaviour was.'

But mixed in with my fear of her, as far back as I can remember, I have also been conscious of her sacrifice (which is perhaps not unlike so many mothers' sacrifice), of her suffering. Subsequently, I've felt tremendous guilt at my own sadness (which felt wasteful, and unjustified, and evidence of my ingratitude) and my own happiness, too (which felt somehow tactless).

My mother was always disparaging of kids who threw tantrums, whom she would call 'manipulative', and instead praised my composure. I don't know if she ever wondered where my anger went, what I was supposed to do with it ... it always seemed like there was enough of hers to go round. M has on occasion said to me, in the midst of my sobbing, 'Why can't you just be *angry* with me? Hit me if you like! Pull out *my* hair!' Jessica Friedmann, talking about her postpartum depression, says that when her son was a toddler, she had to *teach* him how to throw a tantrum; when he got angry, he would just curl up into a little ball on the floor and weep.

It is only recently, in my thirties, I have learned that it is natural for everyone to feel a range of emotions; that everyone feels anger, for example, and that it's important to learn how to express it. I had always conceived of my feelings as things that would overcome me, incapacitate me, and I always thought of this as a deficiency in me. I wanted to feel as little as possible, and I thought that not feeling anything was my ultimate aim.

I want to say that as a child and even as a teenager I wasn't aware of being *unhappy* ... But what I see in hindsight is that I had a lid for all the feeling simmering away beneath the surface (what in therapy-speak gets called a 'coping mechanism') in the form of my studies. It is impossible to overstate how obsessive I was about my schoolwork. It didn't matter what the subject was; I needed to put in maximum effort, and I equated anything less than a perfect score with failure. I attended an academically selective school, and even within that environment of bright kids, I needed to distinguish myself through my marks, which I saw as evidence of my discipline, my potential, the success that awaited me as an adult. Our school motto was *altiora peto* – strive for the highest – and it didn't occur to me not to take it literally.

I never saw it in these terms, but my homework and assessments were also the perfect alibi for me to detach myself from my family – both physically (I was always in my room) and emotionally. I remember in 2003 my mother had to have an emergency appendectomy and this fact barely touched me, because I had an assignment due around the same time. I was, if I'm honest, annoyed at having to visit her in hospital. (I remember afterwards, she told us how another woman in her ward had remarked how very 'cold' I was, so much so that when I entered the room it was obvious I could barely bring myself to touch her.)

My obedience, my perfectionism, my single-minded focus, my self-sufficiency, my will – all of these made for the ideal student. I had no idea, then, the extent to which the sealed world of school was holding me together. Chris Fleming writes that school, with its 'ironclad hierarchies, solid identities, priorities and anxieties, all of them consuming' had fabricated a world that 'at the time seemed indistinguishable from reality itself'. So enculturated into this world was he, that he never appreciated its fragile nature: 'how deeply arbitrary, how quickly it could vanish'.

But vanish it did. 'The objective standards that I'd previously met so well, those marks and rankings, fell away, and I couldn't figure out how to measure myself without them,' writes Fiona Wright, in her memoir's final chapter, 'In

Hindsight'. I remember when reading this chapter of hers, in 2015, that same uncanny shock of recognition I had felt back in 2004 when I discovered that my own compulsions had a name. The same alarming sense of fitting a pattern. With the sheltered world of school vanishing, 'it's so simple a step for hunger to come to inhabit this void'. For me, the first year of university was when my hair-pulling compulsions took serious hold. Fiona again: 'Anorexia has rituals, rules and structure; I know that part of what confused me in my first year at university was the complete absence of these things.'

Part of the appeal of my pulling was how it simplified and structured my life. I was forever calculating: how much I'd pulled that day already; how much more I could afford to pull and still be able to conceal my hair loss. In conversation I'd assess where the light sources were and which angle to therefore hold my head at so as not to expose my scalp; and even when I was in the midst of pulling, my mind was busy making resolutions to stop. There was a steady rhythm to my illness, too: the rising tension and resistance; the relinquishing; the struggle against the ensuing fatigue; the determined holding out to the next binge.

Maura Kelly describes her illness as a 'replacement religion, with its own set of commandments and rituals'. She's referring to her anorexia, though similar sentiments are often expressed by those who pull their hair (in fact, there are high rates of trichotillomania and dermatillomania among anorexics, though nobody understands why). 'My calculations not only filled up all the empty spaces in my head; they also helped me determine the value of my self. On any day I'd eaten less, worked out longer, or lost more, it didn't mean I was *good*, but at least I wasn't bad.' Similarly, on any day I'd pulled too much, I deemed myself a failure, and on any day I'd resisted, I felt a sense of tremendous accomplishment. Resisting pulling became the new thing for me to devote myself to and excel at. (At the same time, paradoxically, that I excelled at pulling, took it to an extreme.)

'Sometimes lately, soon as I wake up, the urges are so so intense. And then I know the entire day is going to be a struggle.'

'So what do you do in that situation?'

'I try to focus on getting dressed, have my breakfast, try to move on.'

'Ah, so you try to avoid the feelings, you want to ignore them.'

'Yeah, I guess so.'

'See I think you need to label those feelings, reflect on why you're experiencing those feelings.'

'But I reflect so much, I'm constantly reflecting and analysing why I feel the way I do.'

'At the time, though?'

'No, normally afterwards.'

'After the event.'

Before I commenced therapy, I was used to thinking of myself as someone very in touch with her innermost feelings. And I thought of my urges to pull as rising up of their own accord, with zero correspondence to my internal state.

Now, I see how severed I have always been from my own feelings: I find it effortful and perplexing to so much as label what it is I'm feeling at any given point in time. When I transitioned from childhood to adulthood, the gaping void left by my studies was filled with pulling. I was a child who studied, who became an adult who pulled. I took both things too far. I'm unable, still, to so much as contemplate *not* going straight to pull that whatever underlying feelings are there get pushed aside. Hands foraging ... and before I know it, I'm in too deep.

Again and again, for all our surface differences, it is the desire to avoid feeling that unifies so many of the accounts of mental illness I read. Jamison: 'My problem was simple but insoluble: I didn't want to feel what I was feeling.' Fleming writes that the drug addict's real problem is not drugs, but being without them: at some point, 'straight reality had become unacceptably angular to me — all sharp edges'. His therapist: 'You're not here to feel better ... you're here to get better at feeling.' Wright, learning to live without her hunger, is stunned at the range of emotions that surface: it is like a 'second adolescence'.

Psychologist Hugh Grubb writes that when emotions are felt to be intolerable, an individual will seek to eliminate them from their emotional vocabulary, and to restrict awareness of them. Hair-pulling provides a 'substitute sense of being connected, and its ritualistic aspect creates a sense of soothing order rather than chaos'. It is a return to the body, but simultaneously a turning away 'both from the rest of the world and from the rest of oneself'.

In the early 2000s (which, coincidentally, was when I began university, and when my compulsions took root), Fred Penzel introduced the stimulus regulation model of trichotillomania, based on his work with patients. He frames pulling as an external attempt to regulate an internal state of sensory imbalance. 'It is as if the person is standing in the centre of a seesaw, or on a high-wire, with overstimulation on one side, and understimulation on the other, and must lean in either direction (by pulling) at different times, to remain balanced,' he writes. This image clarified so much for me, explaining why my triggers for pulling were, on the surface, contradictory: when I'd just received disappointing news but also when I'd received excellent news; when I was overwhelmed by work on weekdays but also when I didn't have much to do on weekends; when I was sleepy but also when I was over-caffeinated.

The suspension of consciousness associated with the trance state provides a space in which one doesn't think about what one feels, and doesn't act on what one feels. A secure, dependable, magical place.

Before each of my sessions I rack my brains for something to say – what is the incident that I should recount, that will be most replete with meaning; what is *the* deepest insight I've had over the week. This becomes so overwhelming a pursuit that often I end up sitting in silence, rigid with panic, pleading with my therapist to suggest a topic for conversation, which she refuses to do. She reassures me, again and again, that if I want to sit there in silence then that is perfectly okay. I'm like a tap screwed tight.

'I don't know what to tell you.'

Her analysing even this: 'I feel like I'm dominating, that I'm in control. It's not about what I want to hear, it's about what you need to express.'

'But I don't want to express anything. I can't. I've always been like this.'

'Adele, you know, you can say whatever enters your head. You could tell me something about your week, or about a book you've been reading ... it really doesn't matter. I think we've talked before, too, about how you seem to think this is only a space to share problems and worries? You can also talk about good things, achievements ...'

'Yeah, that's not my tendency. I guess I'd see it as a kind of boasting, or gloating.'

'And what would be wrong with that?' she asks, ever-Socratic.

Once there is nothing left to pick of my nails, I manage to destroy several tissues within the space of many of these fifty-minute sessions. I barely make eye contact, fixating instead on my creation-slash-destruction: twisting the tissue strips into ropes, then tugging at each until it breaks, unrolling it, re-rolling into smaller snakes, tugging again, then shredding it. Sniffling like a kid who's been sent to the principal's office.

My rigid perfectionism, she points out, makes me so brutal towards myself, so punishing. When I attempt to stop, instead of forgiving myself for the small slips and relapses that I know, intellectually, are 'all part of the process', I berate myself for having failed. When I try out a new strategy, it seems I need to do it with perfect efficiency or not at all. Instead of seeing forgiveness as helpful, I see it leading me into a slippery downward spiral of surrendering entirely to the compulsions ...

But, painfully slowly, I start to learn that there is, ultimately, no right or wrong thing to say. It doesn't matter where I begin, or whether I contradict myself, or repeat myself. It's all 'grist for the mill', she likes to remind me. And nor is there any right way to recover.

'But I can't help but think of you as having a ... a vast picture of human psychology. You're the expert at identifying people's problems.'

'I'm not sure I'd use the word "problems"? I think it can be good for us to recognise patterns, and assess whether those patterns are helpful or perhaps not so helpful.'

'Okay, but surely you have an idea of what would be most productive for us to talk about – you might see a thread we've been following, or see I'm on the verge of something, or ...'

'Adele, *you're* the expert of you. You're the one living your life in the two weeks between our appointments – so whatever you talk about will follow a thread from your life.'

And this lesson helps me with my writing, too: there is no single right way to tell this story, this one that I am trying to relate to you. Where does a story begin? asks Rebecca Solnit. 'The fiction is that they do, and end, rather than that the stuff of a story is just a cup of water scooped from the sea and poured back into it.'

*

When I tell my psychologist about the process of stroking, letting my fingers wander around the scalp looking for something long enough to get some purchase on, she says 'like you're searching for something' and I know she means this not just literally; that she is seeing it as symbolic. And when I tell her about needing to ingest the roots, she asks what it is about the roots that appeals to me; why they are my 'goal'.

Whenever I get into the specifics of the condition she will ask, predictably, why it is *I* do such and such, what it means to *me* personally. Why do I keep this secret? Why am I so terrified of exposure?

Rather than recognising the hallmarks of this disease, she looks for explanations in my own past, unable to understand that maybe there is no meaning behind it – that perhaps I am performing this specific strange ritual because I am used to performing this specific strange ritual, or because I'm no longer able not to.

Frustrated, I tell her if someone came to a doctor with a virus, it would be weird to home in on one symptom and tell the person: *It doesn't matter if other people with viruses also have a sore throat, I want to know what the sore throat means to* you.

But it is so difficult to untangle, where the 'me' is in all this; what's mine and what isn't; which parts mean something and which don't.

How I long for definite answers: to know for sure the original source of my illness; to know exactly the function of my pulling; to be able to trace a definite line between my disease and the rest of 'me'.

Miletic reminds us that one symptom can have multiple meanings. And the more a symptom is present, the more layers of meaning it accrues. (He uses the term 'excavating' for the layers of meaning that can be exposed through the therapeutic process.) What's more, these meanings are not necessarily stable, and can evolve over time. When it comes to trichotillomania, he says: 'We can see in the single act of hand reaching for hair not just a simple movement, but: a coping mechanism; a reminder of something; a message to someone'. I might add: a punishment; a reward; a return to self; an escape from self; a salve.

At some points, when I'm doing all the right things – exercising regularly; eating well; going to therapy; taking a new medication; self-monitoring – and my pulling has been unusually manageable, then I always want to *know*: which of the things is responsible for making the difference? But when I express this desire to my therapist, she asks: 'But what does it matter? Why does it need to be one thing and not another? Why can't it be the combination that's good for you?' It matters because the stretches of time when my compulsions weaken their grip on me feel so very precious, and so promising. I want to know what ingredients are essential, and in what measure, so that I might replicate the result.

Other points, when I'm doing all the right things, and my pulling has been catastrophic, she reminds me: 'There's no *formula*, Adele, for getting better.'

Part of me still isn't quite ready to believe her.

*

Those who suffer from trichotillomania are likely to also suffer from anxiety and depression (the three are what is called, creepily, 'co-morbid'). What is less clear is whether underlying depression might lead an individual to begin pulling, or whether it is the hair-pulling itself (and the shame and isolation that accompany it) that depresses a person's mood.

Is mental illness causative to pulling? Or is pulling causative to mental illness? These two poles underpin the standard treatment models, but each model turns the other on its head. The TLC Foundation for Body-Focused Repetitive Behaviors (BFRBs) disputes the assumption that hair-pulling is a 'sign of some unresolved issue or problem that needs to be addressed for the BFRB to get better', claiming that such behaviours are 'not generally an indication of deeper issues or unresolved trauma'. Trichstop (the go-to online therapy program for those with BFRBs), conversely, frames hair-pulling as 'a mental health disorder ... that results in physical injury'.

And this reflects the curious schism in medicine more broadly between physical and mental illnesses. Which reflects, more broadly still, our cultural separation of body and mind into two unrelated systems. As though thinking and feeling don't both always happen through the body.

When my mother is diagnosed with Stage III melanoma, she says she thinks a lot of people's so-called mental troubles must actually be a sign of something gone wrong in their bodies. That they are depressed, for instance, because there is a cancer growing within them that they are not yet consciously aware of. My millennial sister contradicts her – it is having poor mental health, and a negative mindset, that leads people to have physical ills. They are at odds: *this* way round is the right way round; no, it's obviously not *that* way. As if it's a T-shirt they're talking about, one that's lost its label so that none of us can tell front from back.

Increasingly, I don't see one as leading directly to the other, but the two as cyclical, feeding into one another. In my case, perhaps some undercurrent of anxiety has always been a part of me, and it manifested in me biting my nails and later tearing out my hair, which made me ashamed, which kept me at a distance from other people, which exacerbated the negative feelings I had about myself, feelings I then attempted to relieve through the soothing rituals of pulling, which escalated and heightened my anxiety, ad infinitum.

Such an analysis is so clinical, though, so unsatisfying. Personally I prefer to picture the looping tangles as an image from my very favourite story as a child: *Little Black Sambo* (originally published in 1899, the book is a product of its time). At the end of the book, the tigers – who have claimed items of Sambo's clothing and are arguing over which of them is the 'grandest' – spin round in circles until they become a blur to the eye. (In the copy I had as a child, the up-to-that-point carefully illustrated creatures dissolve, their edges indistinct.)

'They were so angry they would not let go of each other's tail. They were so angry that they ran round and round the tree to eat each other up. Faster and faster they ran until they were whirling around the tree so fast that you couldn't see their legs at all. They ran faster and faster till they all just melted away and there was nothing left but a great big pool of melted butter around the foot of the tree.'

The butter is collected by Sambo's father, and carried home to Sambo's mother, who uses it to cook pancakes. (This detail delighted me as a child, since in my family, it was my father who was renowned for making pancakes.) Being okay with this great big pool of melted butter has turned out to be part of the task of my therapy.

On the Mayo Clinic's website (a US academic medical centre focused on serious, complex illness), I find this explanation for why people pull their hair, perfectly capturing both the internal logic and the pure insanity at the heart of this disease: 'Some people pull their hair intentionally to relieve tension or distress — for example, pulling hair out to get relief from the overwhelming urge to pull hair.'

I had always characterised my childhood as idyllic. And so I struggled with therapy in the first few years because it contradicted this version of events. It has taken me a long time to understand that everything I believed *was*, and was true, but that there was another layer to my existence, too — my childhood was joyful *and* damaging.

My therapist and I talk about how it's possible for different versions of my story to exist. That I'll have my version and my parents will have theirs, and neither of them is right or wrong.

My parents were devoted to me and to my sister. I could always feel, in among my fear of my mother, her unbending love. That evening of the too-salty soup, it is easy to portray my mother as a domineering matriarch. But there was another reality, too.

At the end of a long day's work, it was she who had cooked our dinner from scratch – we almost never ate things from packets or tins. She would have carefully timed the meal so that I would go to my piano lesson with a full stomach. I remember, too, how she'd make soup at those times of the month when my braces had been freshly tightened, because she knew it would be too painful for me to eat anything that required chewing. I never thanked her for all this care. I never had the words to acknowledge her, for any of this. I took it as my due, as children are wont to do.

One of my mother's refrains when I was little was that she wanted me to have a job where I could 'use my brain'. Implicit in this, I think, was that she didn't want my body to have to bear the kinds of strains and pressures hers had to.

I remember in mid-high school, she used to quietly apologise for no longer understanding the schoolwork I was doing and not being able to help me more (she herself had left school in Year Ten, had worked since, had had me young) and I think my teenage self probably gloated at her admission. I wonder, now, if in among her deep pride of me, there was something else: something like fear. Did she think I no longer needed her? That I was, in some way, surpassing her? I feel a deep shame, still, that my life now feels so much easier than hers ever was.

*

Towards the end of one of our sessions, my psychologist says: 'I know you're worried about being weird, but I think once you know the full narrative then your story *makes sense*. A lot of clients I see, it's quite common to feel guilt, but it's important to understand you're not trying to apportion blame, you're just trying to understand. You see, all this hurt goes back: your mother has her own story, her own trauma, as would your grandmother, and so on ...'

It's new to me, and fascinating, to think that it might be possible to trace an invisible line (however tenuous) from me, to my parents, and to their own parents. My father (whose wide-ranging multi-lingual vocabulary doesn't include words like 'depression' or 'PTSD' or 'intergenerational trauma') once said that there was a 'deep sadness' about men of his father's generation, a sadness that 'never seemed to leave them'. I forget now, whether he was talking about his own father, or about my mother's father, who had, we knew, come close to dying in the war, but who never talked about it until in his later years, he grew paranoid, his buried past surfacing in nightly nightmares from within which he would cry out, howling in pain.

So much silence, so much hurt, so much submerged history ... and perhaps some reverberation of it in my body, in my hand, in this gesture that I don't know I will ever be able to bury.

*

Wherever the origins of my illness may lie, and whatever the functions of my compulsions may be, there is still a kernel to my illness that feels beyond analysis. I can feel my impulse to fill in this gap, to settle on the most likely explanation, but there would be something false about that, and so here I want to honour that beyondness, rather than offer you something in its place.

What I have never succeeded in communicating to anyone is that my pulling has become a world of its own, self-sustaining and autonomous. And understanding the question of *why* has, as I write this, done little to dent this world. The more time I dwell in that world, the less important or relevant the question of *why* becomes.

In his account of his daughter's bipolar disorder, Michael Greenberg writes that today it is 'something of a sacrilege to speak of insanity as anything but the chemical brain disease that on one level it is'. But 'there were moments with my daughter when I had the distressed sense of being in the presence of a rare force of nature, such as a great blizzard or flood: destructive, but in its way astounding too'.

For all my copious reading on the subject of mental illness, this is one of the only references I find to the wonder of the thing. For to me there is still an unassailable magic: that in removing a part of my physical self, and then returning it – foreign body delivered to my body – I am able to conjure another world from thin air. 'There is another world and it is in this one,' wrote Paul Eluard, and this is a truth I know inside out.

Pulling is a turning away from the world, but

simultaneously a turning towards another one.

Destructive, but also, in its own warped way, creative.

# M

It's crazy to me now to think that I managed to hide this part of my life, this part of my *body*, from the series of boyfriends that followed my first. And maybe crazier still that I have no memory of any of them – not even once – expressing any kind of curiosity about why, even when we spent our days in one another's pockets, shared plates and socks and toothbrushes and beds, they had never once witnessed me with my hair undone?

Was it their male oblivion? Or was it that I exuded an impenetrability that made such an enquiry impossible?

I can't remember, now, what propelled me to tell M, or how I phrased it when I did. All I remember is him telling me that he already knew. I didn't ask him to explain how, or since when ... I didn't want to know.

I didn't know the reaction I needed until I received it: he told me that when he was a child, he used to pull out his eyelashes. And also that he bit his nails, and even though it wasn't extreme or anything, his mother took him to see a doctor. It was surprising, he said, that someone like her – who hadn't been to school and didn't know the first thing about psychology – should have had such presence of mind, and that she hadn't dismissed his habits as some childish phase.

I hadn't ever told anyone my secret before, but in my imagining – which was as important to me as so-called 'reality' – I could picture people's disgust, or maybe even worse: their advice. But on M's face I detected no discomfort, no pity. He didn't exacerbate my shame in any way, but nor did he attempt to alleviate it. And in this, I saw that he understood perfectly the gravity of my situation.

He told me these things: that it didn't detract from my beauty. That it didn't change anything between us. That he would support me any way he could, any way I asked him to.

When he touched my hair from that point on, it felt doubly tender. I found it strange that I couldn't sense any disgust, in the way that I thought his touch would betray. I really am like a cat. I don't trust strangers, bristle if they try to come too close to me, and past lovers had learned quickly not to stroke my hair at all, in the way that most cats teach you they don't like their tails to be touched.

Growing up we had this one cat, Whisper. Tiny and skittish, when we picked her up from the rescue centre we were told she had been maltreated as a kitten. For years I took secret pride in being the only creature (apart from my sister) whom she trusted; I knew exactly which posture and gaze to adopt that not only allowed me to approach her, but encouraged her to come to me. When I, eventually, learn to trust M, it makes me feel he must possess a similar power. He has managed to soften and gentle me; he is my Adele-whisperer.

I had long thought of the hypervigilance and deception my condition required as being a barrier to intimacy. But now I saw another dimension to my secret: its disclosure could be a means of *offering* intimacy. 'There was my disfigured soul mirrored in my skin,' writes Joanne Limburg of her own excoriated body, 'and if anyone could see it and accept it, then they would accept and understand me totally and utterly ... I had to keep trying, to make that comprehensive confession and get my complete absolution'. Before confessing, I was on one side, and M, along with everyone else in existence, on the other. Afterwards, it felt to me like he'd crossed over: my secret knowledge was now his, too.

My sense of chronology around this is hazy, but I remember there was a good chunk of time when I'd vaguely allude to my pulling, to explain to him why I was tense, or tired, or why I didn't want to stay home alone. If I'd had a bad day, I was able to tell him and he would know to hug me, and the mere fact of being able to do this felt enormous to me.

There was also a period where, at the end of days, I would report to him the specifics of how I had pulled or managed not to. 'Pain is always new to the sufferer,' wrote the nineteenth-century writer Alphonse Daudet in his account of living with syphilis. Each episode in those days felt to me so significant and singular to be recounted and unravelled in all its original detail.

The narrating of my daily struggles must surely have

struck M as monotonous. For those unafflicted, writes Daudet, pain 'loses its originality': 'Everyone will get used to it except me.'

I don't know at what point he told me if I wanted it badly enough, I would be able to stop. I don't know at what point he learned not to say that, to add it to the collection of things that, if he uttered them aloud, would wound me.

Anyone who knows me well knows I have always felt most at ease alone. Solitude feels to me the default, natural state, and I find it trying to be in the presence of most other people. This inclination must have started in my early childhood, when, in the years before my sister came into the world, I never spent one day in preschool, and was largely left to my own devices (back when the word had a different meaning to the one it does now). It is, in part, why the prospect of being a writer appeals to me. And pulling, too, I suppose.

And if my solitary nature led me to begin pulling, then surely, in turn, my pulling had a say in who would become my lover. I find it unnerving to think that *it* exerted as much agency in the matter as *I* did (though, truth be told, I still don't know where the line is, between it and me).

I would never, even without this affliction, have been drawn to the kind of man who sorts women into 'blondes' and 'brunettes'. I suppose if my illness has influenced the kind of men I have let get close to me, it is only to intensify those qualities I already looked for: someone kind, who could carry the weight of my sorrows; someone who knew just the right distance to keep, and who would not deny me my need for periodic solitude; someone who – if it came down to it – could keep a secret.

Since my affliction has taken root, it has poisoned my natural solitude, so that where I ought to feel safest, most at ease, most *myself* has become the riskiest state of all.

I have never pulled in front of anybody. That has always, always been one of the features of this thing. My physical aloneness feels to me not just conducive, but as essential to the act as the dexterity of my own fingers. Even at home, I will always pull out of sight – in the bathroom, or behind a bedroom door. Many times I've been doubled over, frenzied, and it has creeped me out, to think that there is a housemate maybe a metre away in space, and just a fibro wall between us.

How vicious it is, this curse of mine. When I am afflicted, or spent, I find it hard to *be* around other people at all. But nor am I at liberty to be alone, because that leaves me vulnerable to my urges descending.

And so this is where M comes in, for in his presence alone do I feel wholly safe.

Once, he asked me if I ever get frustrated with him, his presence in the room, because it stops me from being able to pull (like an obstacle to my true desire). The truth is I hadn't thought of it like that. His body in the room and his gaze did not just suppress the urges, but seemed to plug them. When he was beside me, I was led to believe that the urges had evaporated.

As *soon* as he was no longer there in the room, though, the urges came rushing straight up.

*

Sometimes, when I've been pulling and am expecting M home at a particular time, there *is* an opportunity to stop, to give myself a little window of time to tidy myself up (in the way I picture 1950s women putting their makeup on to greet their husbands when they walk through the door) but instead of even attempting to stop I keep going, draw it out, because ... because what? I want him to *see*.

Knausgård , having newly completed the writing of a novel of his life, writes: 'but I was not finished with what I had experienced, that is, the place where I felt I had been'. Yes, I thought, that is how it is when an episode has 'finished': I am still there, in that place I have been dwelling.

Sometimes, if I have been pulling badly, and I make it out into public, take up my window seat at the library, open up my laptop, sip at my double-shot latte, all of it (the library, the laptop, the latte) feels like a lie. No other word for it. Because it is so very far from the truth that I have just escaped, and that nobody can see.

And so, in that small window of time when M is about to get home, my options will present themselves like this: You've already been pulling eighty minutes: do you want all this to be invisible to the world? Better to pull just a little more, just five minutes more, and then he will be home, and he will stop you, and then at least this (you?) will be *seen*. To stop and sweep up everything up now would feel its own kind of deception.

For someone so desperately in need of help, is it wrong

to have come to like this feeling of being rescued? To finally, momentarily, be made to feel safe?

The geography of our lounge room is such that each time M prays, his back is to me (towards Mecca, or, by my internal compass, facing the Blue Mountains). Obviously he doesn't have any say in this, and I'd feel like a weirdo – I mean, moreso than usual – squeezing into the narrow space between him and the wall.

Without his gaze upon me, his prayer times come to represent fixed little pockets of temptation. Things can't escalate; I will be forced to stop before he finishes. I find it so strange to think that those points in the day when so many devote their attention to their god should correspond to those points when I turn to the rituals of my scalp.

More than once when I've started pulling in these moments, he will pause his prayer – which he's not meant to do – because somehow, he can nearly always *tell* when I'm doing it. Wordlessly, I convey apology, and he conveys his reassurance. He will usher me into the shower, stand there until my head is under the water because he knows only too well that otherwise I'd stand bunched up against the wall of the shower recess, pulling away until the hot water ran out, and I'd emerge from the bathroom, hair dry; both of us defeated. Then he will slide the glass door shut, and return to his prayer.

In his unbending care, he reminds me of how when I was little, I'd often wake with aching legs – 'growing pains' the doctor called them – and it was my father I'd call out for in the middle of the night. 'Pa-pa? Pa-pa?' and he'd come into my room and I'd flip onto my stomach, bunch up my pyjama pants, and then he'd pour a drop of Goanna Oil into the small hollows of my knees, and rub with his hands, the friction so hard they burned with eucalypt heat, and when the burning got too much, that would be the signal for him to stop, and then he'd tuck me in again, and I'd return to sleep.

Then, as now, all I needed was this: to be trusted that this was not done of my own free will; that the damage was not my fault.

Sometimes, M tells me, even though he knows I don't believe in God, even though I might find it silly, sometimes he prays for me: that I will get better.

Whether I am in public, or in my own home, it has become second nature to me to keep track of precisely who is where, and to know whether I am in their field of vision, to know which doors are open, all so I know whether I can pull without being caught. I have developed the hearing of an animal. If M is in our little kitchen, I can tell from the sounds and silences (in combination with the tips of the shadows that fall that direction in the evenings) when he is still, when he is waiting for something to come to the boil, when he is checking his phone, when he is searching for some spice he can't find.

And he, in turn, is keeping track of me. Despite all its shapeshifting, he comes to understand the precise contours of my affliction through all its ebbs and flows, develops an instinct for it; learns not only to sense when I am pulling, but also when I have been or when I am just about to.

One period I remember the particular contortion of my pulling was such that it would present in the mornings, violently so, and I would struggle to leave my room, struggle to leave the house. He would be at work already by the time I woke, and so he would call at a set time. He would say: *Put the phone down while you get undressed, and then let me know, and then I won't hang up until I hear the shower*. Then he'd call ten minutes later, and I'd narrate to him my putting my shoes on, walking down the stairs, and he wouldn't let me go until he'd heard the sound of the door close behind me.

Once, I remember he was next to me on the bed in the room and it was nearly dark, but not quite, and mid conversation some kind of residual panic returned to me, and he caught it, so quickly ... I think maybe he was talking and I was listening, but he noticed, the exact second my mind wandered. Whatever it was that gave me away, even under almost-darkness he could detect it, sure as a metal detector.

Maria Tumarkin: 'The noticing. Some people are preternaturally good at it. Nothing escapes their eyes it seems. To be seen right through by that one person – is this not one of the great, unspoken human needs.' It is true that I needed nothing more, back then, than for him to *see* me, to see into the marrow of me. But contained in that need was the seed of a new fear: that without him, I would never be seen again.

*

The walls in our apartment building are thin enough that we can hear the exaggerated yawns of the man living opposite; the person above us with their curiously lengthy urinating; the hurling of abuse from across the road: 'slut', 'white dog', 'maggot'. We take advantage of these walls to develop our own secret system of communication, for when a housemate or a guest is in the house. Without us ever discussing it, he develops a throat-clearing kind of cough, and we both know its meaning: 'If you're pulling, now is the time to stop. Are you okay? I am here.' Sometimes when I am in the bathroom and he senses I am pulling, he will tap his fingers on the wall. I wonder, or more accurately try *not* to wonder, what our flatmates and guests make of these curious little exchanges and noises.

In this collusion, it is like the two us are covering not just for *me* but also for *it*. Not just to outsiders, but even with one another. Like, we are doing it a favour, so that it can maintain its anonymity.

For a long time I thought of my pulling (both my physical experience of it, and all the attendant subterfuge) as the most defining thing about me. And M's kindness and acceptance in the face of this was the thing, therefore, I cherished most about him.

But his protection sometimes also becomes — paradoxically — its own invitation to pull. It feels *safe* to pull when he is in the next room, because I know he is there to stop me. It feels *safe* to pull when I know he is on his way home, because I have a parcel of time that I know will be interrupted by his arrival.

Such is the power of my pulling that it has the capacity to twist even his kindness into something fraught.

If my illness is the invisible glue connecting us, then what would it mean were we to take it out of the equation? How could I receive his tenderness if I no longer required it?

Megan Nolan on the possession of her own unspeakable secret: 'I felt a thudding within me, the pure horrifying loneliness of being the only one in the world who knew; the only one except him, of course – and that connecting strand between us danced mockingly, alive and visceral as an umbilical cord.'

I can't conceive of myself without my secret illness, but I can't conceive of *us* without it either.

I am still entangled in this web as I write this. Sometimes I worry M will think I'm using my afflictions to my own advantage. I am addicted to his help, and mightn't he wonder whether my pulling is a means of keeping him close; anchored to me, stopping him from straying?

But that way of framing things assumes that we – we two humans – are the key players here. That way of framing things denies the power of this disease, which has come to feel like its own entity. (Would it be too much of a stretch to say it operates as though it had its own consciousness?)

It has never felt like I was manipulating M, subconsciously or otherwise. My compulsions were always manipulating me;

manipulating us; always one step ahead, so that even the power of two human brains combined were no match for *it*.

When M is not around – whether for a period of hours, or days, or even months – I can, believe it or not, feel safer. Without him around the corner to swoop in to the rescue, I need to be more cautious, need to take all the precautions I can (the memory always looming of what I am capable of disintegrating into).

When we are apart a short time, I think: *Imagine how good it will feel to be able to tell him you managed, you didn't pull at all*. If it's an extended amount of time, I imagine him returning to me not having pulled the whole time he's been away, how nice it will feel to have him touch my un-scratchy scalp.

But then, I think: *Maybe he'll think I don't need him, and I do. I think: I can't just stop pulling, imagine how that will look – I need to pull at least a little bit, to show him some evidence*. Evidence of what? Of my pain? Of how much I missed him? That he mustn't leave me?

'I felt sorry for myself,' says Leslie Jamison, reflecting on her drinking, and its place in her own relationship. 'Now I look back and feel sorry for him, with this girl showing up at his place to cook her rubbery chicken and demanding his compliments in return, then sobbing in his bathroom, clearly wanting *something* from him, but what? Neither one of us knew.'

This question haunts me still: what *is* it I want from him?

Sometimes, I think, the answer is this: Some part of me wants, mid-act, to be *caught*.

When he 'catches' me, with hair stuck around my mouth,

I feel like our cat Minouchette, when she used to stride into the kitchen with a mouthful of feathers, all breezy like nothing had happened. Or not. Did she, at some level, want us to know what she had done? Was it possible to read in her feline expression some complicated mix of guilt and pride?

One night I was on our lounge that sits right by the front door, pulling intermittently over the course of an hour, in that familiar fragile state, skin thin as an eggshell's, and I was waiting for M to come home. In this state I am ultra-alert, still but set to pounce – listening for the engines, checking through the dark the approximate size and shape of each vehicle to see if it could be him. I knew that as soon as M walked through that door he'd be able to tell, even if I wasn't in the act, so to speak.

Anyway, the curious thing was this: that even in this state of semi-delirium, at some level I knew that my composure would be modulated according to who it was walked through that door. If it was a housemate, I'd be able to trick her; to summon up a few seconds of cheeriness, and enough small talk to last until she reached her bedroom door. And if it was M, I would immediately dissolve into tears.

It would be easy to say that one of these reactions was authentic, the other just a mask. But that's not how it felt. Both felt natural, and true.

My disease brings the deepest parts of us both to the surface, and forces them into contact. My despair, my bottomless need. His patience, his forgiveness, his faith. But my fragility tests the limits of his strength and of his patience.

I discern the limits first in his face: not annoyed, exactly, but resolved, like the practised expression a teacher might wear with a kid she knows is volatile, and who she mustn't react to.

When I tell him he's getting tired of me, he assures me he's not. But adds that if I keep repeating this, it might become a self-fulfilling prophecy.

Once, I remember coming home from dinner with friends. I came home in a lighter mood than when I'd left the house, but instead of being pleased, I could tell he was annoyed. Later he confessed he couldn't help wondering: 'Why does she have to save all her sadness for me?'

Sometimes if I get teary, he stops bothering to even ask what the matter is; it's too obvious he doesn't want to be near me, he turns away from me, and this turning frightens me. Sometimes he avoids meeting my eyes, avoids looking at my face at all. Then I hang on every second for him to finally look at me, and with every second he doesn't, I feel worse and worse.

I have no patience for his impatience with me. Which is to say: I demand he see all of my darkness, but I don't allow him his. I show him all my human flaws, but I don't permit him his.

'When darkness engulfed your mother,' writes Knausgård to his daughter, 'when the pain and anxiety swept through her like an avalanche and she lay motionless on the sofa or the bed, I began to ignore it, in a kind of hope that some way or other she would realise that only she could drag herself out of it.' *Oh God*, I thought, when I read these lines. *Does M think his comfort is only fuel for my sufferings?* And more disturbingly: might this be true?

A new terror: that he is only staying with me because of my endless need; that he knows I couldn't survive otherwise. And that I am locked into pulling because it is the surest way of receiving his goodness.

One evening, on our little balcony I confess all this to him. This secret, I tell him, is the heart of how we relate to one another. It is what makes me feel so *close* to him. What would it mean, if it vanished?

And he said: 'It doesn't make me feel close to you. I would much rather you be happy.'

As though all this is not complicated enough: I start to hide my compulsions, like I did at the start, before he knew. A test of two things now: of my powers of deception, but also of his capacity to read my illness (which I have come to see as a measure of how deeply he's able to read *me*).

My routines become even more absurdly elaborate. In the kitchen, for instance, it is hard – if you are in there for genuine kitchen-reasons – *not* to make any noise. If I stand there pulling, then M will recognise the quality of the silence. So now what I'll do, if I'm putting away dry dishes, let's say, is put away one plate, making sure it makes an adequate platey noise, and then pull a little, then a saucer, then pull a little, then a glass, pull, and so on, so that there is a string of sounds to deceive him. Surely this is what craziness looks like?

*

More often than I'd like, I lie to him, say that I'm okay.

Sometimes I admit to him that maybe I'm not getting better, just better at hiding from him, and he assures me he knows this. And I will get used to that very particular look of his: disappointment in me; renewed trust in his own intuition. (I don't know whether he is readier to trust his own razor-sharp instincts, or my word. I am not sure which he would rather be the more reliable.) So many layers and folds of ... of what? Lying? Understanding?

I lie so as not to disappoint him, or cause him worry. I have done enough damage to myself, why damage him as well? Why damage *us*?

I have learned to intuit when he has patience for me and when he does not, and mete out my revelations accordingly. For so long, he has protected me. Now, I want to shield *him*.

When M stops commenting on my hair (whether its growth or its damage) I can't help but interpret this as a sign that he has stopped noticing me; stopped seeing me. I am fully conscious of the irony here: I don't want anyone else to notice anything different about my hair (and I fish for M's reassurance that this is the case), but desire the opposite from him.

I convince myself of my hair's passability, but at some other level am aware that it *does* look weird. A disjointed kind of thinking: I need to believe M has a different level of vision to other people.

Once, I remember saying to him: 'I wish people were more

observant, I wish people would notice all my movements, because that would limit my pulling.' He said: 'But they *do* notice.' Once, he said, my cousins were there, and I pulled a hair at the table, and fed it into my mouth, and one of them saw. M imitated the face he made, and I did my best to suppress the memory of it.

When I complain to M about not making progress he always reassures me that I *am*. That before when he finished work he would have to come straight home to make sure I was okay: 'It was twenty-four-seven,' he says, 'but now it's not like that.'

When my sister and I were growing, our father would periodically mark and date our heights on a section of doorframe, a task we all seemed to take quite seriously.

The way M and I follow the shape and lifespan of my illness is something like the opposite of that.

We try our best to stunt it. We spend more and more time drinking in this feeling, whatever it is you call the opposite of nostalgia.

# SECRECY/EXPOSURE

As a rule, whenever I go bushwalking I avoid taking any photos, no matter how spectacular the view. I have on occasion tried, and the results always make me squirm with discomfort. The images feel somehow a betrayal. I don't like anyone to look at an image of a gorge or a sky and assess its beauty, or to presume to know where it is I have been. And for many years I felt the same unease and resistance in writing about my illness, even to myself. (Let alone to you – you, my mother; you, my stranger).

I have over a decade's worth of journals that make no mention of my secret, don't even allude to it, despite the fact that in those years my compulsions were all-occupying. I wanted to keep tight hold of the closeted, condensed force within me. Wanted to keep my secret pure and *alive*, not flatten it out onto the page.

In hindsight, perhaps there was an element of denial, too, in my writerly reticence. 'I believe that something becomes true if it is spoken,' writes Knausgård , not sharing with anyone his fear that there is something wrong with his newborn daughter, with her faraway gaze. 'If it isn't spoken, it is as if it doesn't quite exist. And if it doesn't quite exist, it hasn't become fixed, and if it hasn't become fixed, it can still go away.'

When in 2018, I finally attempted to put my secret into words – to acknowledge its already-fixed existence – I at first found it physically impossible. I purchased a special separate journal (cloth-bound, ivory-coloured acid-free paper) expressly for the task, devoted a hiding spot to it in my room (double-plastic-bagged, at the bottom of a cardboard box of op-shop-bound clothes under my bed) and even then, it took me several pages of stalling to so much as mention the thing. As though this secret was not just unspeakable, but un-writeable, too.

For the years spanning 2018–2020 I kept two diaries at once: the one that nobody was allowed to open; the second, that nobody was allowed to know existed.

Concealing all trace of my second, secret diary was a natural extension of the impulse that meant I was careful not to ever be seen with too harsh a light shining on my scalp; the same impulse that meant I removed any remnant hairs from the bathroom sink each time I'd pulled. I was so very ashamed of my attachment to such a warped way of living, if living is indeed the right word.

Another explanation for my guardedness: I needed to

keep my illness contained. I refused to let it take up any more space than it already had. I saw my compulsions to write and my compulsions to pull as two distinct spheres, and I wanted to keep my writing (even if destined for my eyes only) a space apart; a space where I could shape a better and more normal version of myself. Australian writer Fiona Murphy, who hid her own deafness for over twenty-five years, admits to the 'thrill' she would feel in successfully passing as 'normal'. The impulse to hide might strike you as meek or cowardly. But like Fiona, I found it thrilling; powerful, too: 'The more I hid my deafness, the more it felt like I had beaten it.'

Writing down what I had deemed un-writeable felt to me a great transgression. My scalp was proof enough of my wrongness, but now even more evidence was amassing, in paper form.

I wish I could say the words streamed out of me; alas, they did not. Apart from anything else, my pulling was a constant interruption to my attempts to write. This was both in a bodily sense – since the two processes involve hands they are physically incompatible – but also mentally. My hands scurrying around my scalp were a sort of flinching from the paralysis that the task of confession provoked in me. The conditions most conducive to writing and creation – solitude, a decent stretch of unscheduled time – felt volatile, ripe as they were for self-destruction. In trying to lure the muse, I was also luring whatever it was in me that compelled me to pull.

'The space between me and everyone else seemed to swell,' writes Jessie Cole, reflecting on what compelled her to begin disclosing her own secrets in written form. The more permanent my own state of secrecy came to feel, the more distant I, too, felt from other people. 'When I started writing,' says Cole, 'it was not an act of sharing with others but a kind of joining of my outside self with my hidden inside ... There was no reader. There was only me and me. I was whispering secrets in my own ear.' This is how it was for me, too. I would write just a line or two at a time – as though I was in an old-fashioned library, and needed to be careful to limit myself to hushed sounds.

When it came to pulling, the removal of individual hairs always felt insignificant enough that there was mostly no visible change perceptible before and after any one episode. But over time, whole startling zones devoid of any hair would emerge. Trying to put words to the experience of my illness was so painstaking and so incremental a process that it was sometimes hard to trust I was really *creating* anything. And when I began to knit the various fragments together into some loose form, it involved so much backtracking and deletion. Eventually, though, things did start to fall into place, and whole startling zones of prose emerged.

In other words, both processes were accretive and piecemeal, but they moved towards opposite ends.

Earlier, I told you that for a long time, I was intent on keeping my secret intact within me, adamant that any attempt to write about it would destroy its wholeness. I can't really account for the shift; all I know is that another need in me grew: for my secret to take up some kind of space in the world outside my own body. Outside my mind, my scalp, my fingertips.

I believed that only through writing could I overcome my illness once and for all. I believe this still. I don't mean I think of writing as a straightforward cure, nor even that it is 'therapeutic' in the way some people like to claim. But that doesn't mean that writing is *nothing*. For me, writing is an admission that my illness cannot be made to disappear into thin air (science has never been my forte, but isn't this the case for any kind of matter?) The best I can hope for is for it to be displaced. Writing is an attempt to displace (or purge?) my secrets out of my body and onto paper. So that they still have a home.

The more I wrote about my secret illness, the more I needed to write. The more I wrote, the more I began to feel I was regaining control. The writer James Bradley – himself prone to depression – rejects both the (widely spouted) idea that 'being disturbed makes one a writer' and, relatedly, that 'to be a writer one must be disturbed'. Rather, he says, the 'peculiar pressures associated with mood disorders, the emotional lability and sense of the fragility of the self, the swings and uncertainties in mood, the vulnerability to stress and personal trauma' give birth in many writers to the compulsion to 'control and order the often unbearable pressure of day-to-day existence through the controlling medium of art'. I was so used to being held captive to my illness, to it structuring and dictating my choices, that it felt good to be able to try to capture *it*, to impose structure over it. A way to come into power, and a kind of weak revenge I suppose, for all it has stolen from me.

At first, the only way I could bear to write about my illness was to believe that reader and writer alike were 'me and me'. I needed to banish the censorious eyes that were always hovering over my shoulder. But, of course, as Rebecca Solnit puts it, a book 'exists fully only in the act of being read; and its real home is inside the head of the reader'. A book is 'a heart that only beats in the chest of another'.

To be able to write any of this I had to pretend that you – you, my mother – would never set eyes on it. But secretly I was also writing this *for* you, so that you could understand.

I recall once, maybe a year ago, you told me and E both that when you were pregnant with each of us, privately you hoped that you didn't have boys, and you were glad when we were both born girls, because you were afraid of whatever it was in the males in your family – your own brother, and then there was a cousin of yours, too, and Nana's brothers, and her father. You said you didn't want to have to 'deal with all that'. You said it to us, as though E and I had made it through unscathed.

When I showed E the opening chapter of this book, she barely commented on its content. 'What will Mama say?'; she looked as protective of you in that moment as you usually do us.

I told her: if *I* were my mother (if I were anyone's mother) then I would want to *know* this about my daughter; I wouldn't want for her to wait for me to die before she felt safe to voice her secrets.

And you, my stranger, I am also writing this for you. It is just like Solnit says: when it comes to matters 'so subtle, so personal, so obscure' – 'Every once in a while I try to say them aloud and find that what turns to mush in my mouth or falls short of their ears can be written down for total strangers.' It is because of you I have been able to write any of this: you 'the absent, the faraway, the not yet born, the unknown, and the long gone for whom writers write, the crowd of the absent who hover all around the desk'. It is because of you that I have begun to un-swell the space between me and everyone else.

The more I listen to my impulse to write about my illness, the more my pulling is coming to feel justified. A kind of research, or fieldwork.

When I am at that critical point, first hair ready, on the verge, lately the voice that doesn't ever feel delivered in words but as something more instinctive says: *Go on! Then you can write about it!* And then once things – predictably – start to escalate, I think: the more intense the episode, the better, because surely fresh raw pain will be excellent meat for writing?

And so in addition to the usual fear, that I'm never going to banish my animal urges, lately when I have an episode I fear, too, that this will be the last time, and that its memory will vanish, like all the others have.

And so I think: *Not yet, don't stop yet, you're not ready, the writing's not ready for it, your writing will run dry.* There's an intensity and a specificity to that place I go when I pull that I'm terrified I'm incapable of ever capturing adequately.

Rebecca Solnit frames writing as an attempt to 'preserve something that might otherwise vanish'. The act of writing 'fixes a story in its particulate, like the apricots fixed in their sweet syrup ... And what is left out is left out forever'. I keep on pulling, because I'm so very afraid of what I might leave out. I want to be freed of my illness, but I can't bear the thought of it vanishing without trace.

The thought of ever publishing these words troubles me, since in this age of googling, even those who don't ever lay hands on my book will be able to discover my secret at the click of a couple of buttons. The digital spectre of my double-plastic-bagged-under-my-bed secret walking around inside their pockets.

But here's the crazy thing. Compared to my terror of anyone discovering my secret in what we call 'real life', the thought of strangers discovering my secret doesn't terrify me in the way I imagine it probably should.

What comforts me is this: my secret, obsessive mindscape is capacious; so much so that I could never reveal all of it to you, no matter how hard I tried. And so I feel safe in the knowledge that so much of my secret world is still mine; still there for me to tap. Helen Garner – master of self-scrutiny – admits feeling surprise when people 'express appalled amazement' about what they consider her 'self-exposure'. 'One of my sisters, a nurse, told me that when she read my story "Spy in the House of Excrement", about the Thai health spa where one fasted and took enemas twice a day, she wanted to "pull the screen around me". But I don't feel exposed, because in this mysterious way I'm trying to describe, the "I" in the story is never completely me.' How utterly perfect this observation. I spent so long frustrated that my writing could never capture my experience completely, but now I take solace in that same fact. You can never know my secret completely, because the 'I' in this story I'm telling you is never completely me.

What's more, I imagine that what has happened to me is not mine alone; is not incomprehensible to you. My hope is that you will be carried through what Garner calls 'the superficial levels of perviness' and 'urged into the depths of (your)selves'. 'I hope that we can meet and know each other there, further down, where each of us connects with every other person who has ever loved or been loved, hurt and been wounded.'

To mark my mother's fifty-seventh birthday, the four of us spent a long weekend at Pittwater YHA, set on a steep hillside above a bay in Ku-ring-gai National Park, and only accessible by ferry. It was the sort of unpretentious place we all liked: a great big verandah; close to bushwalks and swimming spots; a kitchen so we could make our own meals; birdlife everywhere: cunning kookaburras, and cockatoos the exact same pristine colours as the frangipani on which they perched, and then down at the water: pelicans and cormorants and osprey.

We had the place virtually to ourselves: just a pair of Korean backpackers and one other family there – one of those Northern Beaches families that radiate good health, the sort who send their kids to Montessori schools and shop at organic farmers' markets.

On the Saturday we went walking, and afterwards we curled up and read novels in one another's company, and I made a blue cheese and caramelised onion quiche for dinner, and my mother looked happy, and through it all I seethed. On the Sunday the others wanted to try out the kayaks, which I knew would leave me feeling even more trapped, so I told them in as casual a voice as I was able to muster that I was feeling tired and I might just stay and read my book. Mama asked whether I was okay, and was it just the dental anaesthetic from the filling I'd had on Saturday still wearing off? I really was tired, though, and on edge as a result, since tiredness was the surest way for my urges to emerge, and so while they were out on the water, I slept.

On the Monday E was heading back early afternoon because she had to be at work Tuesday. She said she'd get the three o'clock ferry. I was so exhausted (despite having slept in) and ashamed of this exhaustion, needed desperately to disrupt it somehow, so I told her I'd go for a swim at the spot where the kayaks were docked – even though I'd not been there I'd seen the little turnoff – and then meet her at the wharf in time to say goodbye, which was fully my intention at the time, and hardly an ambitious plan. I had a good forty-five minutes up my sleeve. And so I set out, feeling blurry and not quite there, but hopeful that the water would wake me.

The place, when I eventually got there, was not how I'd envisaged it. Deserted, and no canoes in sight. I can still picture the wide swathe of grassland and no real track to reach the water, but a path made by virtue of people walking through it, the grass leaning either side, neatly parted.

I made my way to the water, sat on the thin strip of coarse sand, removed my hat. It felt less risky to pull here, both because nobody was watching and because the water was *right there* – it would only take a few seconds to dunk my head under and thereby provide myself a window of time in which I wouldn't be able to pull ... The sun was at its highest, a fact that meant my head was heating up, which meant the roots of my hair would soften, and slide out like butter, and be slightly stickier, *wet* almost. And warm against my lip, like something warm-blooded.

And so the next hour – or two? – passed. My wide-brimmed hat beside me, my hairpiece stuffed inside its bowl, and me alone with my compulsions. Hairs falling onto the sand, tumbling gently onto the water's surface and carried away by the tide's own pull.

Now, it's the mangroves I remember most. How within that episode they took on a lucidity. Not morphed into anything else, just plainly and clearly themselves. The gnarled, irregular corkscrew twists not quite spiralling, but so like the kinks of my own hair (when the shaft gets damaged then the regrown hair will grow at a slight angle, instead of straight upward and out, like it's meant to, and this is what produces the kinks). It was odd I'd never seen the resemblance before: the roots all roughly the same height, but not quite. I mean, not like if someone shaves their head, then all the regrowth is even, obviously – here, some patches were denser, some sparser, and the individual protrusions slightly different lengths and thicknesses, some stunted-looking, some more tapered, some only just emerging from the earth, which from the angle I was sitting had the perfect curve of a scalp.

The fact I'd just spent two hours good as paralysed washed over me. None of this registered as all that remarkable any more. Inch by inch, I thought, my life had come to this; my daily, routine experience so far removed from what other people understood reality to be.

I remember being struck by the sensation that this was an *event*, discrete, and occurring at a particular time. And the event connected me to this place. That it remained unspoken, and that I was the only one to know about it, this only made it feel all the more important. Intimate is perhaps the best word for it, in the way that if knowledge is shared by two people alone it's lent a significance. Except this was a secret between me and the mangroves.

Mostly I conceived of my secret as one great ugly lump. But each time something like this happened, I saw that my enormous secret was actually made up of thousands of smaller ones, that each required their own specific suppressing.

When I eventually managed to make my way back up

the slope towards the hostel, I spotted my parents coming downhill, not quite hand in hand but close by one another, and my father's face was strangely painted with worry, and at the sight of them, and at the sight of their faces lighting up at the sight of me, I was filled with sudden tenderness for them, for their love, for the fact that I was theirs.

'Ça va ma grande? You missed saying goodbye to E, and then we were starting to worry you might have got lost!'

'No, no. I just had a nice long swim.'

And the three of us headed back up the hill.

I went to my room, 'to get changed', but once there I couldn't stop the tears.

I went to find Mama, because I knew I would have to at some point. We returned to the room I'd been sharing with my sister, and I lay down on the double bed, facing the wall, and she lay behind me, came closer, and put her arm around me.

'Ever since I got here I just feel so anxious, like ... I can't get calm.'

'Yeah, I thought something might be wrong, when you didn't want to come canoeing with us.'

'I just feel like I'm really not good company, and I didn't want to spoil your birthday.'

'Oh, don't be silly. Have you got any idea what might be making you anxious? Are you and M having relationship problems?'

'No. It's not that. I ... I don't know how to tell you, because I don't want to hurt you. But the reality is that ... I feel anxious around you, Mama. Which I know is unfair. Like, today I can see clearly that you're not stressed, and you're in a good mood and everything, but still when I'm around you I just can't help feeling so tense ... and then I feel guilty about it, because I know it's not your fault ... and then that makes me feel even worse.'

She pulled closer, so her breasts were pressed gently against my back.

'Oh, Adele. It sounds just like how I used to be around Nana.'

'I feel so silly.'

'Don't feel silly. I'm glad you could tell me. Are you ... are you able to talk to someone about it?'

'Yeah, I've been seeing a psychologist actually. She's really helpful.'

'Oh that's good, I'm glad you're seeing someone.'

We lay there some more like that, wordlessly, and I felt ... not unburdened, but *softened*. I thought, for a moment, of removing the hairpiece, which would only take a second, and flinging it across the bed, and letting her see the shock of my scalp, its growth as insubstantial as lanugo, that fine fur we all once possessed, when each of us was still swimming inside our mothers.

But then I thought better of it: I didn't think I could bear to hurt her.

'Did you want to come and have some tea, or some of that lemon tart?'

'I don't want Papa to see me like this, though. He'll just start laughing at me.' I loved being the object of my father's affection, and could not bear the thought of becoming the object of the ridicule that I had always known him to heap on those he deemed unduly sensitive, or delicate, or plaintive. Or self-absorbed.

'No he won't.' She said it like he would never do that; like she knew him best; like I must have mixed him up with some other person. I only had one father, that much I knew. But in moments like these, when my mother was made of kindness, I wondered whether I had two mothers, and whether the other one, the one whose anger haunted me, was now gone.

On the ferry back to Church Point, it was just us and that other family with their branch-like limbs ... the girl on her mother's lap out the front in the open air, legs dangling. When she spotted her dad and her brother get up to use the bathroom, she sprang up and raced after them like she was scared to miss out.

I pressed my face against the window, tried to let the sight of the water calm me. Not far below its surface I could see jellyfish bobbing, dozens upon dozens of little translucent spheres, their tentacles so fine as to be invisible, even from this short distance. I studied the watery surface, here buckled by the ferry's body, there slightly crepey, like the skin of warmed milk, and then, a little further out, all taut-looking. A partition between two worlds.

I'm telling you this, about the ferry and the jellyfish, because these are the kinds of moments that helped me, and help me still; that remind me that, despite everything, the world is still here, alive and astounding, letting me watch, and listen. The world is waiting patiently, for me to be ready to return.

And I, too, have been waiting, not quite so patiently, for my disease to be over, to leave me please, so that I might be returned to the world ... though sometimes, lately, I see that actually, more and more of me *is* here, however fleetingly, however tenuously, and however shyly.

Some writing guides say that the best writing sounds like someone is speaking. You should be aiming in your writing to capture the quality of spoken speech, and when editing your writing, you should read it out loud. But what if the reason you're writing the words in the first place is that it's impossible for you to speak them?

'The tongue fails where the fingers succeed, in telling truths so lengthy and nuanced that they are almost impossible aloud,' writes Solnit. When my fingers succeed in removing the hairs from my head, I discard them to the floor, to the bin. When my fingers transmit the words from inside my head to the page, I can't know who will eventually receive them. There is something terrifying about this, this ultimate and irreversible exposure, but something thrilling, too, a deep thrill it is impossible for me to admit to out loud.

# ACKNOWLEDGEMENTS

Over the course of writing this book, Virginia Center for the Creative Arts, Booranga Writers' Centre, and Varuna National Writers' House all provided me shelter, and the fellowship of other writers. Thanks especially to Veechi Stuart and Amy Sambrooke at Varuna, for your mountainous hospitality.

Create NSW and the Copyright Agency's Cultural Fund helped me to fund mentorships with a trio of excellent women: Carol Major, Fiona Wright, and Tegan Bennett Daylight. Carol: thank you for appreciating the strange, repetitive beauty of my illness, and for connecting it to the patterns of all living things. Fiona: it's your writing that first taught me how to write about experiences which are not linear; which are aberrant and unresolved. I cherish your company, both on the page and in our local coffee shops. Tegan: thank you for your immense generosity and sensitivity, your readerly prowess, and for taking me under your wing.

To Gaby Naher: thank you for inviting me to join your circle, for your kindness, and for handling all the parts of the publishing process that I know nothing about.

Thank you to all the wonderful team behind the scenes at Scribe Australia & UK, who have made me feel in such safe hands.

Marika Webb-Pullman: thank you for agreeing to publish my work, and for taking such tender and meticulous care of my sentences.

Thanks to Laura Thomas for a cover more beautiful than I could ever have imagined.

I abandoned the writing of this book countless times. Thanks to M, for always gently persuading me to persist, and for being with me through thick and thin.

Thanks to my sister, for being such a good sister. I hope you might read this one day.

To my parents: thank you for reading this book through to the end. I know that your doing so has already brought us closer. Thank you for having the humility and the grace to wish this book well, as it travels into the world.

# FURTHER READING


### CHAPTER 1

D.H. Lawrence, *The Rainbow*, Methuen & Co., 1915.

### CHAPTER 2

Rebecca Solnit, *The Faraway Nearby*, Viking Books, 2013.

### CHAPTER 3

Tim Winton, *The Boy Behind the Curtain*, Penguin Books, 2013.

### CHAPTER 7

Anthony Synnott, *Shame & Glory: a sociology of hair*, *The British Journal of Sociology*: 38, 1987.

Lee Kofman, *Imperfect*, Affirm Press, 2019.

Mary Douglas, *Purity and Danger: an analysis of concepts of pollution and taboo*, Routledge & Kegan Paul, 1966.

**CHAPTER 8**

Judith Rapoport, *The Boy Who Couldn't Stop Washing*, E.P. Dutton, 1989.

Violet Media, *My Strange Addiction*, Season 1 Episode 6, 2011.

Fred Penzel, *The Hair-Pulling Problem*, Oxford University Press, 2003.

Guadalupe Nettel (translated by Rahul Bery), 'Bezoar', *Granta* (online), 2015.

The Mariana Enríquez quote is an endorsement of Guadalupe Nettel's *Bezoar & Other Unsettling Stories* (translated by Suzanne Jill Levine), Seven Stories Press, 2020. For an extended video conversation between Nettel and Enríquez, see *Louisiana Channel's* 'The Dark and the Hidden', 2019.

**CHAPTER 10**

Leslie Jamison, *The Recovering: intoxication and its aftermath*, 2018.

Fiona Wright, *Small Acts of Disappearance*, Giramondo, 2015.

**CHAPTER 11**

Karl Ove Knausgård (translated by Ingvild Burkey), *Autumn*, Penguin, 2017.

Susan Sontag, *Illness as Metaphor*, Farrar, Straus & Giroux, 1978.

For further information regarding randomised controlled studies of EMDR therapy, refer to: emdrfoundation.org/emdr-info/research-lists/.

Eleanor Limburg, *The Woman Who Thought Too Much*, Atlantic Books, 2010.

Esmé Weijun Wang, *The Collected Schizophrenias*, Graywolf Press, 2019.

Chris Fleming, *On Drugs*, Giramondo, 2019.

Hilde Bruch, *The Golden Cage: the enigma of anorexia nervosa*, Harvard University Press, 1978.

Louise Glück in Kate Taylor (ed.), *Going Hungry*, Knopf Doubleday, 2008.

Rebecca Solnit, *The Faraway Nearby*, Viking Books, 2013.

For a series of freely accessible lectures on trichotillomania, created by Dr. Vladimir Miletić, go to: trichstop.com/webinar.

Maura Kelly in Kate Taylor (ed.), *Going Hungry*, Knopf Doubleday, 2008.

Hugh Grubb, 'Awakening from the Trance', TLC Foundation website: bfrb.org/articles/awakening-from-the-trance

Quotes from the TLC Foundation, Trichstop, and the Mayo Clinic are all taken from these organisations' respective websites.

Helen Bannerman, *Little Black Sambo*, Grant Richards, 1899.

Jessica Friedmann's observations are taken from an event she conducted with Fiona Wright & Roanna Gonsalves at UNSW in 2019: 'UNSWriting: The New Essay: illness, place, and reinvention'.

**CHAPTER 12**

Alphonse Daudet (translated by Julian Barnes), *In the Land of Pain*, 2002.

Karl Ove Knausgård (translated by Don Bartlett), *My Struggle Book 2*, Farrar, Strauss & Giroux, 2014

Maria Tumarkin, *Axiomatic*, Brow Books, 2018.

Megan Nolan, My Eyes! My Eyes!', first published on *Medium*, now available via *Roulette* (Substack)

Karl Ove Knausgård (translated by Ingvild Burkey), *Spring*, Penguin Books, 2019.

**CHAPTER 13**

Fiona Murphy, *The Shape of Sound*, Text Publishing, 2021.

Jessie Cole, *Staying*, Text Publishing, 2018.

James Bradley, 'Never Real and Always True: on depression and creativity', *Griffith Review 23*, 2009.

Helen Garner, 'I', *Meanjin 61.1*, 2002.